# Antigua and Barbuda

Cavendish Square

New York

Published in 2022 by Cavendish Square Publishing, LLC
243 5th Avenue, Suite 136, New York, NY 10016

Library of Congress Cataloging-in-Publication Data

Names: Kras, Sara Louise, author. | Nevins, Debbie, author.
Title: Antigua and Barbuda / Sara Louise Kras and Debbie Nevins.
Description: Third edition. | New York : Cavendish Square Publishing,
  [2022] | Series: Cultures of the world | Includes bibliographical
  references and index.
Identifiers: LCCN 2021011031 | ISBN 9781502662750 (library binding) | ISBN
  9781502662767 (ebook)
Subjects: LCSH: Antigua and Barbuda--Juvenile literature.
Classification: LCC F2035 .K73 2022 | DDC 972.974--dc23
LC record available at https://lccn.loc.gov/2021011031

Writers: Sara Louise Kras; Debbie Nevins, third edition
Editor, third edition: Debbie Nevins
Designer, third edition: Jessica Nevins

CPSIA compliance information: Batch #CS22CSQ: For further information contact Cavendish Square Publishing LLC, New York, New York, at 1-877-980-4450.

Printed in the United States of America

Find us on

# CONTENTS

# ANTIGUA AND BARBUDA TODAY

**W**HITE SAND BEACHES, TURQUOISE BLUE WATERS, AND SWAYING palm trees. Warm tropical sun and the exhilarating rhythm of calypso music floating on the breeze. Incredible views of spectacular sunsets from Shirley Heights. Harbors full of white luxury yachts and colorful fishing boats. Pretty little houses painted in pastel colors and friendly people. All of these are reasons why tourists flock to Antigua and Barbuda.

Antigua and Barbuda is a country in the Caribbean Sea—one nation made up of two main islands. Most people live on the island of Antigua, and because the full name of the country can be cumbersome, it is often simply called Antigua. Despite how it is spelled, Antigua is pronounced an-TEE-gah, not an-TEE-gwa. At least, that's how the local people pronounce it, and they should know. (Antigua, the island and nation, is not to be confused with Antigua Guatemala, a city in the central highlands of Guatemala in South America.)

The majority of Antiguans and Barbudans are descendants of enslaved Africans who were forcibly brought to the islands in the 17th century by the British to work on sugar plantations. Although the enslaved people were emancipated in 1834, the

This election billboard urges Antiguans to vote for the Labour candidate Asot Michael. He won reelection in 2018 and became the minister of investment and trade. The Labour Party was founded by V. C. Bird, the nation's first prime minister.

islands remained under the control of Great Britain for another one and a half centuries. After the inhabitants of the islands demanded independence from British rule, democratic elections began in 1980, with the country being led by Vere Cornwall Bird of the Antigua Labour Party. Antigua and Barbuda has since risen from brutal subjugation to freedom and independence after centuries under the yoke of slavery and colonialism.

The sugar trade, the main source of income for Antigua and Barbuda in the past, has since been replaced by tourism. People come from all over the world to visit these pristine islands. Today, this democratic country is known for its safe ports, world-class sailing races, beautiful beaches, and offshore banking.

Antigua is well known as an attractive haven for foreigners' offshore banking needs. Its banking sector is the second-largest in the Eastern Caribbean region. Offshore banking simply means having a bank account outside one's own country. It can be used for personal or corporate financial matters. Typically, people choose to keep their money in a foreign bank for tax reasons—in other words, as a way of avoiding paying taxes at home. More relaxed banking regulations at such offshore sites may also make it easier to shield accounts from scrutiny. It's not illegal, but it can be, as such financial institutions tend to be used for illicit purposes such as money laundering (hiding money obtained through nefarious means). However, stashing secret fortunes isn't quite as easy as it once was; for example, as of 2017, banks in Antigua and Barbuda had to begin reporting banking information of U.S. citizens, in accordance with the United States' Foreign Account Tax Compliance Act.

Very wealthy people live in Antigua, but many of its residents are quite poor. There is a great disparity in wealth between the small upper class and the rest of the nation's people. Much of Antigua's economy is based on catering

to the wealthy, but the government itself has limited resources, which is why many roads are unpaved—especially in the interior—and bumpy with holes and ruts. It's why there is still open sewage in some places, polluting the beautiful environment. It's why the government introduced a citizenship-for-sale scheme in 2013; anyone can become a citizen of Antigua and Barbuda for a donation of $250,000 or a property investment of at least $400,000. It's also why some government officials have been vulnerable to corruption.

In the tug-of-war between nature and development, money often wins. In 1997, then-Prime Minister Lester Bird announced that a group of ecologically sensitive islands just off Antigua's northeastern coast, previously proposed

Houses dot a lush hillside in Saint John's, Antigua, which is sometimes spelled as St. John's.

for national park status, were being turned over to Malaysian developers. The Guiana Island Development Project sparked widespread criticism by environmentalists and the press. The deal called for a 1,000-room hotel, an 18-hole golf course, and a world-class casino to be built there. Emotions ran so high that at one point in 1998, a local resident of Guiana Island, who was being evicted to make way for the development project, shot the prime minister's brother, a member of Parliament. (He survived.) The proposed development subsequently became mired in lawsuits and politics.

The 5-square-mile (13 square kilometer) island was previously owned by the American financier Allen Stanford, once Antigua's biggest investor. His island empire fell apart in 2009 after he was arrested and convicted in the United States of massive fraud. The Antiguan government ended up selling Guiana Island and abutting mainland sites to Chinese developers in an investment deal called the YIDA Project. The island has been deemed a semi-autonomous Special Economic Zone, so, essentially, Antigua sold some of itself to China. The island will be more than just a tourist attraction; it will be a community unto itself with homes, a shipping port, a hospital, schools, and even an industrial section for steel and ceramic tile factories. Construction is well underway.

Antigua's Environmental Awareness Group, the island's largest environmental organization, could only decry losing the protected natural areas. "We have spent 25 years working there, rehabilitating habitats for various wildlife," Arica Hill, the group's executive director, said in 2019. "[Now we're] seeing 25 years of work go downhill. It's literally devastating."

In a very different attempt to obtain financial support for the country, Antigua and Barbuda is seeking reparations from Harvard University Law School. Harvard Law School was established in the early 1800s through a bequest from the estate of Isaac Royall, a wealthy Antiguan plantation owner and enslaver who immigrated to Boston, Massachusetts. In 2019, Prime Minister Gaston Browne argued that the law school was built using riches obtained from the unpaid labor of enslaved people. The descendants of those people are today's Antiguans. The matter remains unresolved.

Those are some of the issues facing Antigua and Barbuda today. Barbuda, in particular, the quieter island, is still rebuilding from near total devastation

in 2017 from Hurricane Irma. Also, in the wake of that disaster, the global COVID-19 pandemic hit Antigua where it hurts most—by pulling the rug out from under the crucial tourism industry.

Climate change, environmental protection, and economic health—today's islanders must grapple with a number of such challenges as the 21st century moves ahead. Meanwhile, life goes along in this island nation under a bright, tropical sun and to a calypso beat.

Uniformed marchers celebrate 39 years of national independence on November 1, 2020, in Saint John's, which is the nation's capital.

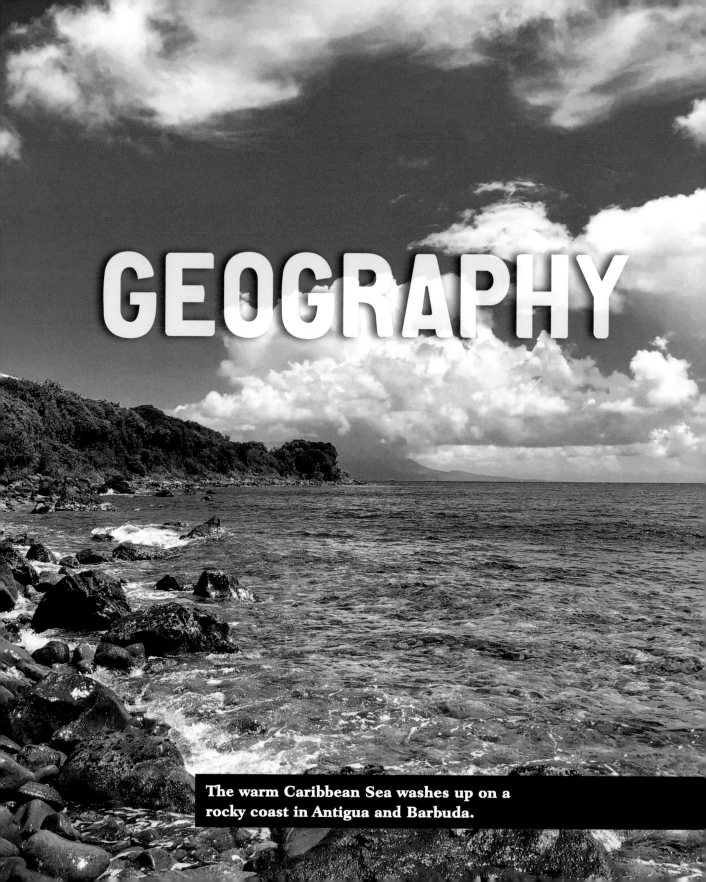

# GEOGRAPHY

The warm Caribbean Sea washes up on a rocky coast in Antigua and Barbuda.

A NTIGUA AND BARBUDA IS ONE country made up of two main islands in the Caribbean Sea. It's located in a larger group of islands called the West Indies, in the Lesser Antilles archipelago.

The Lesser Antilles is a chain of islands that arc between the Greater Antilles islands and the continent of South America. This archipelago contains 24 island states, of which eight are independent nations and the rest are territories of the United Kingdom, France, the Netherlands, or the United States.

Antigua and Barbuda is an independent nation. It covers a total land area of 170 square miles (442 sq km), about 2.5 times the size of Washington, D.C. It lies about 430 miles (692 km) north of Venezuela, a country on the northern coast of South America. In addition to the two main islands, the country also includes Redonda, an uninhabited island that lies 25 miles (40 km) southwest of Antigua. There are also some other outlying islands, including Crump Island, Great Bird, and Guiana.

## ANTIGUA

Antigua is the country's main island, home to 98 percent of the country's population. Geographically, the island was born of volcanic activity, but today it has no active volcanoes. With the passage of time, three distinct land types developed on Antigua—the southwestern volcanic region, the rolling plains in the central section, and the uplands located in the northeastern area. Volcanic sediment can be found to the west,

**English Harbour in Antigua is a beautiful sight from Shirley Heights, one of the island's higher points.**

and limestone plates appear on the east side of the island, almost dividing it in two. Along its white sand coast are many inlets and bays. A large protected harbor called English Harbour is located on the south shore.

Antigua is known for having 365 beaches, one for every day of the year. Its coastline is scattered with numerous bays and coves lined with reefs, along with white sand beaches lapped by crystal blue water. Galley Bay, along the northwest coast of the island, is known for its crashing waves. Next to it is Hawksbill Bay, named after Hawksbill Rock, which is located offshore. The rock resembles the head of a Hawksbill turtle, from which its name was originally derived.

The southwestern and southern coast is scattered with hills. At 1,319 feet (402 meters), Boggy Peak is the island's highest point. It is located in the southwestern corner of Antigua.

On the southern shore is English Harbour. Yachts and boats are often docked in this protected area. Some of the beaches in this area can only be reached by vehicles with four-wheel drive. Located in the hills of the southern coast is green limestone, which is quarried and used for building churches, houses, and roads.

On the east coast of Antigua is Half Moon Bay, a curving bay with a beautiful beach. On the easternmost side of the island is Long Bay, where the water is a clear turquoise blue, and the protected reef is filled with a wide variety of colorful fish. Also in this area is a limestone arch called Devil's Bridge. Milky-white waves carved out this beautiful natural phenomenon over a period of time and now crash through its blowholes and against its volcanic rock. Deep, narrow crevasses line the stony surface from which growling sounds echo, emitted by the treacherous waters below. The arch received the name Devil's Bridge during the time of slavery because so many desperate enslaved people jumped off it to die by suicide. It was thought that the devil was in the area.

**SAINT JOHN'S** Small villages are scattered throughout the island of Antigua. However, the majority of people on the island—around 21,000—live in the capital city of Saint John's. It's located in a sheltered cove on the northwest side of the island. Antigua's main port, Deepwater Harbour, is also located there. The historical town dates to the 17th century, when it became the administrative center for Antigua and Barbuda. Today, it is the capital of the country and the seat of government. Because of the many cruise ships that visit this port, its harbor has been dredged to allow megaships to dock.

Despite its heavy tourist trade, Saint John's still maintains its old-world charm. One of its oldest buildings is the courthouse, which was constructed around 1750. Originally, the courthouse was used by the Supreme Court and the Houses of Parliament. Today, it is used as the Museum of Antigua and Barbuda. Another historical building is Saint John's Cathedral. Its baroque towers dominate the skyline.

In 2009, the prime minister of Antigua and Barbuda at the time, Baldwin Spencer, renamed Antigua's highest peak Mount Obama to honor U.S. president Barack Obama as a symbol of Black achievement. In 2016, the government changed the mountain's name back to its traditional name, Boggy Peak.

Pastel Caribbean colors adorn the buildings of Saint John's. Visible in the background is Saint John's Cathedral.

Throughout the city, there are still several 18th- and 19th-century buildings. Some were houses for plantation owners. Other historical reminders are the metal boot cleaners located next to the sidewalks. They were used hundreds of years ago to scrape mud off boots. During the sugarcane era, the sidewalks were built like stairs with high and low steps. The low steps were for the men, and the high ones were for the women to help them get into a carriage.

The historic Redcliffe Quay was originally used as a holding area for cargo during the 18th century. Goods such as cotton, sugar, sheepskins, and tobacco were held there. This quay also contained a slave-holding compound. Thames Street, beginning at Redcliffe Quay, was where the enslaved people were lined

up and inspected by future enslavers. This event was called "the parade." People would come from all the other islands to attend the parade and purchase new enslaved people. Today, tourists flock to Redcliffe Quay to purchase clothing, jewelry, toys, and other items.

Just a couple of miles outside Saint John's is Fort James. This historical fort contains 10 cannons. Each cannon weighs 2.5 tons (2,449 kilograms) and required 11 men to fire just one shot. Each shot could travel a distance of 1.5 miles (2.41 km). Even so, Fort James was never utilized in battle.

This aerial view shows historic Fort James at the entrance to Saint John's Harbour in Antigua. The fort, named for King James II of England, was built in the 18th century by the British.

A girl holds a handful of tiny pink shells, which make up Barbuda's pink sand beaches.

## BARBUDA

Barbuda is a low-lying coral island about 27 miles (43.5 km) north of Antigua, with its highest point being only 125 feet (38.1 m) above sea level. It's made of ancient coral reefs, limestone, and low-rising sand dunes. On the western side of the island is Codrington Lagoon, which opens up into the sea. The central area of the island is flat, whereas the eastern region has higher tablelands with limestone cliffs and caves. Barbuda has miles and miles of pristine beaches made of white and pink sand. The pink sand is made of crushed conch shells.

Prior to 2017, about 2 percent of the country's people lived on Barbuda, primarily in the village of Codrington. The village was settled as the main residential center of the island in the 17th century. King Charles II granted a 50-year lease to Christopher and John Codrington, powerful landholders, on

June 5, 1685. The Codringtons used the island to make and prepare supplies that were shipped to their plantations in Antigua and other eastern Caribbean islands. Enslaved people had their own small homes in Codrington.

In September 2017, the population of Codrington went from about 1,800 to 0. Hurricane Irma devastated the island, and all residents were evacuated to Antigua. Around 95 percent of the structures on the island were damaged or destroyed. Since then, rebuilding has slowly begun, and some former residents have returned.

## REDONDA

The small island of Redonda is located 35 miles (56 km) southwest of Antigua. It reaches 984 feet (300 m) high and is 0.77 miles (1.25 km) long. Because of the large amount of seabird droppings on the island, Redonda was mined for bird guano, which was used in fertilizers, in the 1860s. Later, aluminum phosphate, a valuable component of gunpowder, was discovered under the guano, so mining operations were established. At one point, about 100 miners worked on Redonda. A cableway using baskets was built to transfer the mined phosphate to a pier for shipping.

After World War I (1914—1918), a small mining crew remained on the rocky island to maintain the equipment. This continued until 1929, when a hurricane destroyed most of the mining buildings. No one lives on the island today.

## CLIMATE

The weather in Antigua and Barbuda is warm and sunny all year long. Even though there is some seasonal change, the average temperature is 81 degrees Fahrenheit (27 degrees Celsius). Because the islands have a tropical climate, temperatures can rise as high as 93°F (33°C) between May and October. However, sea breezes called trade winds help to cool the air.

The annual rainfall is about 40 inches (100 centimeters). The months of August and September usually receive the most rain.

Antigua lies within the hurricane belt, which consists of areas vulnerable to hurricanes. As a result, it has been affected by a number of hurricanes. Hurricane

# HURRICANE IRMA

*On September 6, 2017, Hurricane Irma blew across the Caribbean region, causing catastrophic damage and loss of life. One of the hardest hit islands was Barbuda, where the Category 5 storm reached its peak intensity. A strong storm surge (an abnormal rise of sea water caused by a storm) of about 8 feet (2.4 m) also devastated the low-lying island. A 2-year-old boy died in the storm. Meanwhile, Antigua suffered far less damage and no fatalities. Hurricane Irma went on to cause further destruction and loss of life in other Caribbean islands as well as in Florida. It was one of the strongest Atlantic hurricanes on record.*

*Barbuda was left with no electricity and no drinking water. Two days later, with yet another storm (Hurricane Jose) heading straight for Barbuda, the country's prime minister ordered an evacuation of the island. All 1,800 residents were ferried to Antigua, leaving Barbuda uninhabited for the first time in 300 years. Then, on September 18 of that year, Hurricane Maria, another Category 5 storm, swept across the Caribbean. Although Hurricane Maria caused further damage to Antigua and Barbuda, the worst of its wrath was felt by the islands of Dominica, St. Croix, and Puerto Rico.*

Codrington, Barbuda, was left uninhabitable after Hurricane Irma. Shown here is the aftermath of the storm.

season lasts from July to November. In 2017, Hurricane Irma devastated Barbuda.

## FLORA

It is hard to know the original indigenous plants of Antigua and Barbuda because of the intense colonization during the sugarcane era that stripped the islands of their natural forests. Furthermore, over the years, varieties of plants were introduced into the country's ecology by settlers from different parts of the world. Some of the plants were from neighboring Central and South America, but others came from as far away as Asia and Africa.

A breadfruit tree bears its bumpy fruit. One breadfruit tree can produce up to 450 pounds (200 kg) of fruit each season.

Coconut trees, Cretan date palms, calabash, and breadfruit grow on Antigua and Barbuda. The versatile fruit from the breadfruit tree can be baked, roasted, or made into a casserole. Another useful tree is the tamarind. Its seeds are boiled and dried. They are then used by local women to make placemats, coasters, bracelets, necklaces, and bags that are sold to visiting tourists.

The national tree is the whitewood tree. It is related to almond and mangrove trees. It grows mainly next to dry river beds and in the coastal areas of Antigua. Its wood is very hard and strong and resists decay because it does not rot very easily, even in the humid tropics. In the past, flooring, gates, carts, and benches were made from the whitewood tree. Because of its usefulness, many were chopped down, and today there are very few of these trees left.

Different types of bananas grow here, such as the lady finger banana, which is smaller than a commercial banana and can be eaten in a variety of ways. However, the plantain, another variety of banana, should only be eaten fried or boiled.

A variety of herbal and flowering plants can be found throughout Antigua and Barbuda, such as the seaside grape, black willow, bougainvillea, hibiscus,

## ANTIGUA'S VOLCANIC NEIGHBOR

*The island of Montserrat lies around 30 miles (48 km) southwest of Antigua. In 1996 and 1997, a volcano erupted on the island, completely covering its capital city in ash, huge rocks, and other debris. The hospital, the airport, a Catholic church, and hundreds of residents' homes were totally buried.*

*Even though the city had been completely evacuated a year before the eruption, no one knew for sure when the volcano would explode. Some people began moving back into the capital city prior to the eruption, and 19 people were ultimately killed. After the huge explosion, refugees poured out of Montserrat. To help these refugees, the Antiguan government allowed 3,000 to settle in Antigua, thus swelling its population.*

*During the explosion, some of the ash blew over to Antigua, covering cars and houses with a thick layer of dust. People wore masks to protect their lungs. Small earthquakes shook the streets in Saint John's and outer villages.*

*Since then, the volcano has had other large explosions, one in 2002 and another in 2003, when one of the lava domes collapsed, sending ash up to about 50,000 feet (15 km). In 2010, lava flows destroyed the island's international airport.*

The active Soufriere Hills Volcano in Montserrat, as seen from a helicopter, is shown here.

oleander, candelabra cactus, and barrel cactus. Antigua also has ponds scattered throughout the island that are filled with lotus blossoms.

The national flower of Antigua and Barbuda is the *agave karatto*, a succulent with dagger-like green leaves that grow up to 3 feet (1 m). Its name comes from the Greek *agave* meaning "noble." The agave grows in dry areas, such as the woodland hills. It stores water in the fleshy leaves at its base. Growing from the base are tall flower stalks up to 20 feet (6 m) high. Its golden flowers bloom only once every 10 to 20 years, then die. Another name for this plant is the century plant because it blooms so infrequently.

## FAUNA

There are three distinct types of animals that live in Antigua and Barbuda—animals in the air, on land, and in the water.

In the air, one can find fruit bats and free-tailed bats. Free-tailed bats are the most common. Using echolocation, they find insects and feast on them. Other flying animals are the pelican, cattle egret (locally called *gauling*), osprey,

The rusty plummage of a trio of whistling ducks shines in the bright Antigua sun.

A stag fallow deer shows off its impressive antlers. The deer is pictured on the coats of arms of Antigua and Barbuda.

hummingbird, red-billed tropicbird (locally called *chichichawa*), and whistling duck, known for its sharp whistling sound.

On the ground are mongooses, donkeys, and goats. The mongoose was brought to Jamaica from India in 1872 to kill rats and snakes on sugarcane plantations. Eventually, it was brought to Antigua. Mongooses are seen all over the island of Antigua walking warily across a road or yard. However, there are no mongooses on Barbuda, where they are illegal.

The European fallow deer is the national animal of Antigua. In all the eastern Caribbean countries, deer can only be found on Antigua and Barbuda. This is why it was named the national animal. This deer is not indigenous to Antigua and Barbuda. Instead, its roots are thought to be in England. It was brought to the islands by the Codrington family.

In 1784, there were up to 3,000 deer living on Barbuda, but by 1827, they were considered a pest because they stripped the land of local vegetation. When Bethell Codrington bought Guiana Island, a small island 300 feet (91 m)

*Since 1975, the United Nations Educational, Scientific and Cultural Organization (UNESCO) has maintained a list of international landmarks or regions considered to be of "outstanding value" to the people of the world. Such sites embody the common natural and cultural heritage of humanity, and therefore they deserve particular protection. The organization works with the host country to establish plans for managing and conserving their sites. UNESCO also reports on sites that are in imminent or potential danger of destruction and can offer emergency funds to try to save the property.*

*The organization is continually assessing new sites for inclusion on the World Heritage list. In order to be selected, a site must be of "outstanding universal value" and meet at least one of ten criteria. These required elements include cultural value—that is, artistic, religious, or historical significance—and natural value, including exceptional beauty, unusual natural phenomenon, and scientific importance.*

*As of January 2021, there were 1,121 sites listed: 869 cultural, 213 natural, and 39 mixed (cultural and natural) properties in 167 nations. Of those, 53 were listed as "in danger." Antigua and Barbuda, being such a small country, has only one World Heritage site, a cultural listing called the Antigua Naval Dockyard and Related Archaeological Sites. This group of naval structures and fortifications was built in the English Harbour region by the British navy beginning in the 1700s, using the labor of enslaved African people. The purpose of the compound was to protect the interests of the sugarcane plantation owners at a time when European powers were competing for control of the Caribbean islands. The site has been protected as a national park since 1984 and was designated as a World Heritage site in 2016.*

An old sundial is on display at Nelson's Dockyard, which is part of Antigua and Barbuda's World Heritage site.

from the island of Antigua, deer were taken there to be raised. Currently, this national animal can be found living happily on the Barbuda and Guiana islands in small numbers.

There are several reptiles living on Antigua and Barbuda, such as the land turtle, gecko, tree lizard, racer snake, toad, and tree frog. The land turtle was introduced to Antigua by Native Americans and European settlers. Sailors stored land turtles on their canoes or ships as a constant source of fresh meat on long sea voyages. Today, these turtles are sometimes kept as pets.

A variety of insects and arachnids live on the islands, such as the cicada, horse spider, firefly, and honeybee. The honeybee is not native to Antigua. It was brought over from Europe during the 18th century to provide honey for the islanders. Butterflies are also common. It is not unusual to see hundreds of them flitting through the air.

A tarpon swims in the mangrove shallows in Antigua.

In the surrounding sea live humpback whales, green turtles, barracuda, albacore, groupers, yellow-tailed snappers, flying fish, and dolphins, which can sometimes be seen hunting stingrays leaping out of the water as they try to escape. Tarpon favor the warm, shallow waters just offshore. Corals and shellfish also make the sea their home. In addition, there are lobsters, smooth brain corals, white sea urchins, land crabs, Caribbean oysters, queen conchs, and southern stingrays, which glide through the water like elegant birds. These stingrays measure 6 feet (1 m) from wing tip to wing tip.

In some areas of Barbuda, the beaches are littered with empty queen conch shells. The conch can grow up to 10 inches (25.4 cm) long. This mollusk has a rubbery meat that is a favorite West Indian food. Its shell is lined with a pretty pink and peach color and is often used to decorate yards or houses.

## INTERNET LINKS

**ab.gov.ag/detail_page.php?page=26**
Antigua and Barbuda's national symbols are described on this page.

**www.globalsecurity.org/military/world/caribbean/ac-geography.htm**
This overview of the country's geography includes maps.

**www.theguardian.com/global-development/2017/nov/20/the-night-barbuda-died-how-hurricane-irma-created-a-caribbean-ghost-town**
This article describes the destruction of Barbuda by Hurricane Irma in 2017.

**whc.unesco.org/en/list/1499**
This is the home page of the Antigua Naval Dockyard World Heritage site.

# HISTORY

An old cannon faces the sea at Fort James, at the entrance to the harbor of Saint John's. The fort was built in 1706 to guard the harbor and is one of many forts built by the British in the 18th century.

**2**

LONG BEFORE THE PEOPLE OF EUROPE discovered what they called the "New World," people lived on the islands of the Caribbean. For them, the islands were not only *their* world, but a very old world at that. People have inhabited Antigua since around 2900 BCE. Evidence of early settlements was found near current-day Parhram. Another ancient site that dates back to 1775 BCE was also found in the Jolly Beach area.

On Barbuda, a Stone Age site that dates back to 1875 BCE near Martello Tower was found. Ancient Amerindians lived in Antigua and Barbuda until about 100 BCE.

The Ceramic Age slowly started around 775 BCE when Amerindians from mainland South America, called Arawaks, began to arrive in dugout canoes. They made pottery and were farmers. They planted a variety of crops, such as pineapples, cotton, and peanuts. Their main food staple was the cassava root, which was planted in abundance.

After 1200 CE, a new group of Amerindians arrived, the Caribs. Even though they were warlike, they began mixing with the existing Arawaks. Through this combination a new group called Island Caribs was formed. These were the people living in Antigua and Barbuda when Europeans arrived in the 16th century.

In the 18th century, the number of enslaved people living in Antigua and Barbuda greatly outnumbered the Europeans who held them captive. Today, 87 percent of the population of Antigua and Barbuda is Black, and 4.7 percent is mixed race.

## EUROPEANS ARRIVE

In 1493, Christopher Columbus visited Antigua. He named it after the miracle-working saint of Seville, Santa Maria la Antigua. The Island Caribs already had a name for Antigua—Wadadli, which is still used today by locals.

There is no evidence that Columbus saw Barbuda. After Columbus, both the Spanish and the French attempted to settle there without success because of fierce opposition by the Native people. The first permanent European residents of Antigua were the English, who came from the Caribbean island of St. Kitts in 1632. Once they arrived, they claimed Antigua for the English Crown. This group of people was under the leadership of Sir Thomas Warner, who was instrumental in colonizing many of the Leeward Islands. They established a small settlement with numerous farms. They were attacked at various times by the Island Caribs, as well as the French and Dutch, but the English persisted and became permanent residents. The threat of Island Carib attacks eventually dissipated, as there is no further historical reference to the Island Caribs on Antigua after 1705. Most likely, the population was largely wiped out by smallpox and other European or African diseases.

In the early 1600s, tobacco was the main crop produced on the Leeward Islands. Because tobacco was harmful to the soil, its production was stopped in the mid-1600s. Sugarcane was soon grown in bountiful abundance.

The demand for sugar grew, creating a continuous triangle of trade. Goods such as guns, textiles, and horses were brought from Europe to Africa. These goods were exchanged with the local tribes living along the coasts of Africa for humans to enslave. The enslaved people were then sent to the Caribbean and sold to sugarcane plantation owners at a high price. Payment was usually made in sugar, rum, or molasses; this new cargo was then shipped to Europe and sold at a high profit before the cycle started all over again. The sugar industry was extremely important to the economy of England. Therefore, England needed to protect its interest in the sugar trade against the French and the Spanish. To accomplish this, the British navy established English Harbour and many other forts around the island of Antigua.

## THE SUGARCANE ERA

In 1674, Sir Christopher Codrington arrived from Barbados, where he was a powerful landowner, and established a large sugar plantation on Antigua. He brought in enslaved people from Africa to work on his plantation. He also brought the latest techniques for growing sugarcane and used windmill technology. Because Antigua's land was flat with strong trade winds, it was a prime location for windmills that drove the sugarcane crushers. These huge crushers were originally built out of lignum vitae wood, which was indigenous to Antigua and incredibly strong.

This 1823 engraving by William Clark illustrates how people loaded barrels of rum and sugar onto ships in Antigua.

## HOW SUGARCANE WAS MADE INTO SUGAR

*Once the freshly chopped sugarcane arrived at the mill, it was fed into three heavy rollers and was crushed. Workers were very careful not to get too close to the rollers for fear of a hand or even an arm being completely smashed. The huge sails of the mill moved the crushing rollers about four times a minute. The command "Turn her out!" was used to start the mill, and "Turn her in!" was said to stop it.*

*While the cane passed through the rollers, a green sugar juice would drip into a pan below. The pan dumped into a wooden gutter that led to the boiling house. The leftover crushed stalks were spread out and dried in the sun and were later used to keep the fires going in the boiling house.*

*The enslaved workers who toiled in the hot boiling house removed the impurities in the sugar by adding lime to the sugar juice. The juice was then placed in huge, open cast-iron or copper tanks. The sugar juice was heated until the water evaporated and it became thick like caramel and turned a brown color.*

*The sugar was then spooned into large wood boxes to crystallize. Once it was crystallized, it was taken out of the boxes and placed in wooden barrels or clay pots and put in the curing house to dry for about two to three weeks. After the curing was complete, the sugar was sealed and shipped to Europe to be sold in the markets.*

Enslaved workers plant sugarcane in Antigua in this 1823 illustration by William Clark.

Because of Codrington's financial success, more windmills followed. By 1748, there were around 175 windmills dotting the countryside of Antigua. The remains of some of them can still be found today.

In addition to their sugar plantations, Christopher Codrington and his brother John were given permission by the British monarch to lease the island of Barbuda. The lease was for a set period of time. The rent payment was established as one fat sheep yearly. Christopher Codrington also served as the governor of Antigua from September 1689 to July 1698.

The Codringtons were allowed to renew their lease of Barbuda in 1705 for 99 years. Barbuda was sometimes used as a vacation spot for the Codringtons and their wealthy friends. The island was stocked with deer and boar, so the Codringtons could take their friends on hunting trips. Several hunting lodges were constructed, and their ruins can still be found all over the island today.

Abandoned windmills recall Antigua's history on a former sugarcane plantation.

African and white enslaved people were housed on the island of Barbuda, as well as livestock such as sheep, cattle, hogs, and hens. The enslaved people on Barbuda had different jobs than those on Antigua because there were no sugarcane fields to work in. Punishment for rebellious enslaved people on Barbuda was to be sent to Antigua to work the fields.

Even though Barbuda was not used to grow sugarcane, it was still a very profitable island for the Codringtons. The Atlantic side of the island was surrounded by a shallow reef where passing ships sometimes met their demise. The cargo from shipwrecks earned Codrington a good sum of money, as he could sell it once it was salvaged. To expedite the process and also increase profits, enslaved residents were instructed to place large torches near the reef. Captains of passing ships thought the torches were fires on land. They would steer their vessels toward the fire and crash into the reef. Enslaved people would swim out to the sunken ship and loot its treasures. Ruins of a storage house for salvaged goods can still be found near Two Foot Bay on the northeastern side of the island. Today, 145 shipwrecks have been documented off the coast of Barbuda.

## NELSON'S DOCKYARD

Because of the valuable cargo being shipped to and from the Caribbean, it became the site of a power struggle between Britain, France, Spain, and Portugal. Britain employed the use of its powerful navy to protect its interests in the eastern Caribbean. One of its main naval bases was established in English Harbour, Antigua. It began as a naval dockyard in 1725, when funds were set aside for its construction. The facilities created a safe haven for British ships in the Caribbean. The harbor protected the ships from marauding pirates or

A colonial fortress still stands near Nelson's Dockyard.

## CAREENING THE SHIPS

*Careen means "to lay a ship on its side for repairs," which includes fixing leaks or scraping barnacles off the hull. Nelson's Dockyard was set up to careen large ships. Capstans, cylinders that cables were wound around, were built in Nelson's Dockyard to assist in this process. Several capstan bars or poles were used as levers to wind the cables. All of this was done with manpower. In Nelson's Dockyard, a man was placed between each slot of the capstan bars while a fiddler stood on top of the cylinder. When the winding process started, the fiddler began to play to encourage the men during this hard work.*

*Careening a ship required the following steps:*
*1. Tying a ship to a deep-water wharf*
*2. Removing all heavy and loose objects on board*
*3. Removing the topmasts*
*4. Attaching a framework with rope that was connected to a capstan*
*5. Slowly tilting the ship on its side by winding the capstan*
*6. Repairing one side of the ship's bottom*
*7. Repeating the process for the other side of the ship*

devastating hurricanes. It also served as a ship-repair station—a place where ships could have broken masts rebuilt, sails repaired, and barnacles scraped off their hulls. Repairing royal naval warships was the most important function at the harbor. These ships were used to protect British colonies and capture other sugar islands of the French, Spanish, or Portuguese, which in turn increased the wealth of Britain.

The structures in the dockyard were made of local stone and brick from Europe. The brick was used as ballast in the bottom of incoming ships and was off-loaded at the dockyard to be used as building material. To hold the stones together, the British used sand from the beaches and made mortar. This harbor was known as the best British harbor in the West Indies.

The majority of buildings seen today at the harbor were built between 1785 and 1792. During some of this time (1784–1787), Admiral Horatio Nelson was stationed there. The dockyard was named in his honor and today is known as Nelson's Dockyard.

*Up to the 18th century, Antigua and Barbuda was still in danger of being attacked by pirates. There are many stories of such attacks. One such story is about a pirate named Captain Daniel in the late 17th century. He and his men stormed the island of Barbuda and attacked the Codrington manor. The pirates burned down houses and took 15 enslaved people.*

*The British government received several pleas from its colonies for protection against raiding pirates. Ships attempting to reach Antigua's shores with goods for sale and trade were often attacked by these bandits. One such bandit was the pirate Captain Finn. There was much celebration in Antigua when he and five of his men were hanged in 1723. Afterward, their dead bodies were displayed as a warning along the water's edge to other pirates.*

*Antiguan plantation owners and the British government funded the building of several forts to protect the island. One was called Shirley Heights and was built overlooking the Caribbean Sea. Included in the complex were artillery quarters, officer quarters, a large fort, a cemetery, and a*

An old colonial military complex stands at Shirley Heights, overlooking English Harbour in Antigua.

*hospital. It was used as a lookout for incoming ships. If a ship was spotted, a flag was raised in the air. Through a series of flag systems around the island, Saint John's and the entire island could be alerted within 15 minutes of an incoming ship and whether it was an enemy or friend.*

Many rules were established to keep peace and order on the dockyard. Women were not allowed on the dockyard because they caused distractions, and smoking was not allowed because of the large amounts of gunpowder in the area.

Fort Berkeley, located on a strip of land at the entrance of the harbor, was established to protect the dockyard. Because of these strong fortifications, Antigua was never overtaken by another European power.

In 1961, Nelson's Dockyard was named a historical monument of Antigua, and in 1985, it was established as a national park. Today, it is part of a large national park that includes the Dockyard Museum and the old Admiral's House. In the museum, visitors can view various 18th-century artifacts from battles at sea and raiding pirates. Other buildings that have been restored in the dockyard are the pitch and tar store, the old guard house, the copper and lumber store, and the officer's quarters.

**The view from Shirley Heights looks down on Fort Berkeley, near English Harbour.**

## EMANCIPATION

Throughout the centuries of slavery, there were several uprisings on the two islands. Conditions for the enslaved workers on the nearly 200 plantations of Antigua were unspeakably cruel. In 1736, an enslaved man named Prince Klaas helped plan an insurrection aimed at seizing control from the white minority and establishing an African kingdom on the island. However, Klaas and his fellow plotters were found out and were publicly executed by horrific means as a way of warning against further uprisings. Today, Prince Klaas is celebrated as one of Antigua's greatest heroes.

Finally, in 1834, slavery came to an end in Antigua and Barbuda. This was one year after Great Britain passed an act eradicating slavery throughout its empire. Liberta was the first free village in Antigua and Barbuda, followed by Freetown and Freeman's Village.

Even though the enslaved people had been freed, they still had to earn money to survive, and many had to continue working for the plantation owners. They lived in the same ramshackle huts as before and were forced to work as laborers for inferior pay with very little rights. A worker could be sent to jail and whipped for the smallest offense. In addition, murders of Black workers occurred with very little investigation by the local government to find who was responsible.

Riots broke out a few times, with the offenders shot on the spot by police. Black workers rarely questioned or demanded better treatment from the plantation owners, because if they did, it was highly likely that they or their family would be killed. Nevertheless, conflicts between workers and sugar plantation owners continued throughout the 19th and early 20th centuries.

## INDEPENDENCE

Between 1938 and 1939, Sir Walter Citrine, general secretary of the British Trades Union Congress, who was visiting the West Indies, founded the Antigua Trades and Labour Union. In 1943, Vere Cornwall Bird was elected as the president of the Antigua Trades and Labour Union. This energetic leader fought long and hard for laborers' rights. The labor union eventually became the first

political party formed on the islands in almost 30 years. It was later called the Antigua Labour Party (ALP).

In order to gain independence, Antigua joined the West Indies Federation in January 1958. However, the federation was short-lived and was disbanded in 1962. Antigua gained associated status with Great Britain in February 1967. With this status, Antigua was responsible for its internal affairs and government, whereas Great Britain kept the responsibilities of managing Antigua's defense and foreign affairs. During the 1960s, the sugar industry began to fail, and by 1971, it was completely shut down. In its place, Antigua looked toward the tourism industry as a source of income.

A statue of Sir Vere Cornwall Bird Sr., the first prime minister of Antigua and Barbuda, stands close to the marketplace in Saint John's.

Antigua still sought complete independence from Great Britain. Elections took place in April 1980, and the ALP won. On November 1, 1981, Antigua and Barbuda received their independence, jointly. Vere Cornwall Bird was named the first prime minister of Antigua. Barbuda sent a request to Great Britain to be its own nation, but its request was denied. As a result, the Barbuda's People Movement was formed, which continued to demand secession from Antigua.

Other political parties were formed in this new democracy, such as the United People's Movement, the Barbuda National Party, and the United National Democratic Party. Even so, throughout the 1980s, the ALP, led by the Bird family, was the dominant force in politics.

## CORRUPTION

In the past, there have been accusations of corruption and criminal activity taking place in the government. These came to a head in April 1990, when the government of Antigua and Barbuda received an official letter of protest from the government of Colombia. The letter complained of illegal sales of firearms that were being supplied from Antigua to the drug traffickers in Colombia. A judicial inquiry took place, and Vere Bird Jr. was found guilty and banned from politics for life.

In 1999, the U.S. government issued a report that stated Antiguan banking laws were allowing money laundering, or disguising money from criminal activities. After this report, great efforts were made by the Antiguan government to clean up these allegations and problems.

Corruption continued to plague the government, which included the ALP and the prime minister. In 2001, there were fraud allegations against the minister of health due to his conduct as head of the state-run Medical Benefits Scheme. He resigned, but an independent inquiry took place. The inquiry recommended that the Medical Benefits Scheme become an independent group, separate from the government. It also recommended that a prosecutor be appointed to look at charges brought against 12 people involved in the fraud. The prime minister, Lester Bird, was never directly implicated, but rumors circulated about his possible involvement.

In April 2002, Lester Bird had a public dispute with the leaders of the popular United Progressive Party (UPP). He initiated a libel suit against these men that included the future prime minister, Baldwin Spencer. Lester Bird later dropped the suit.

Allegations of illegal activity mounted in May 2002, when an ALP member of Parliament, from Bird's own party, demanded Lester Bird's resignation, as well as that of his chief of staff. The UPP organized thousands of demonstrators in the streets demanding the same thing. It was not until March 2004 when the Bird family's power was finally usurped in a general election. The United Progressive Party won those 2004 elections, and Baldwin Spencer became the prime minister. Later that same year, Parliament passed an anti-corruption bill aimed at cleaning up governmental fraud and misbehavior.

Ten years later, the ALP regained power with a massive win in 2014, installing Gaston A. Browne as Antigua and Barbuda's new leader. His wife, Maria Bird-Browne, is the niece of the former prime minster Lester Bird. In 2018, she ran for—and won—election to the House of Representatives.

## INTERNET LINKS

**www.bbc.com/news/world-latin-america-18707512**
A timeline of key events in the history of Antigua and Barbuda is presented on this page.

**www.smithsonianmag.com/history/antiguas-disputed-slave-conspiracy-of-1736-117569**
This in-depth article looks at the horrors involving an uprising of enslaved people in 1736 in Antigua.

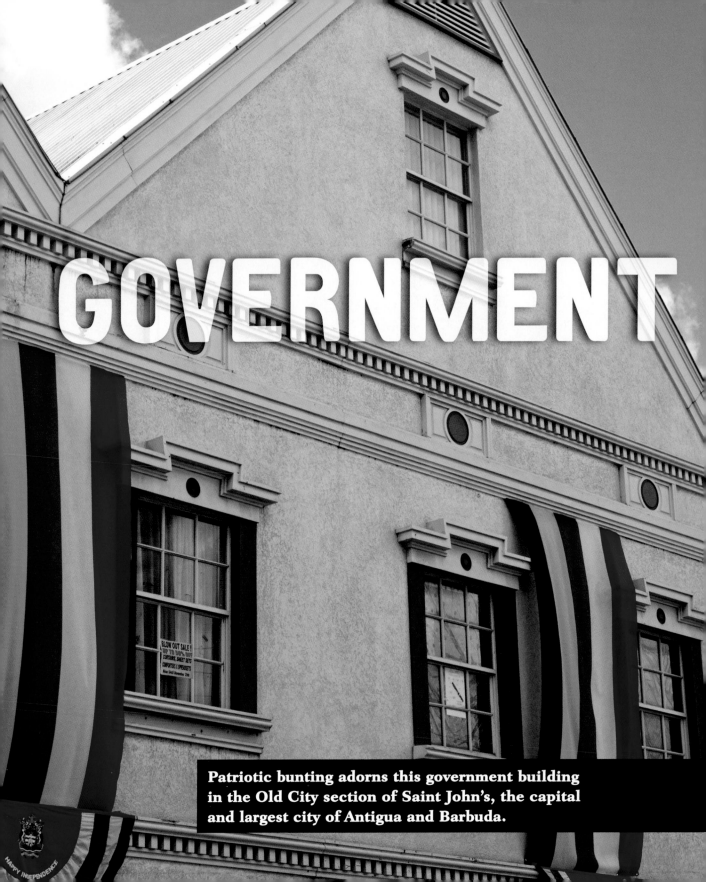

# GOVERNMENT

**Patriotic bunting adorns this government building in the Old City section of Saint John's, the capital and largest city of Antigua and Barbuda.**

# 3

**T**HE REPUBLIC OF ANTIGUA AND Barbuda is a parliamentary democracy under a constitutional monarchy. The capital is Saint John's on the island of Antigua.

Antigua and Barbuda achieved complete independence on November 1, 1981, and today the nation celebrates that date as Independence Day. Although the country is no longer under British colonial rule, it remains a constitutional monarchy. That means the reigning British monarch (as of 2021, Queen Elizabeth) is the nominal head of state, with a governor-general (since 2014, Rodney Williams) appointed as a representative of the monarch. Antigua and Barbuda is also a member of the Commonwealth of Nations, an association of former territories of the British Empire. Antigua's British-style government system has three branches: executive, legislative, and judicial.

## THE CONSTITUTION

The Constitution of Antigua and Barbuda was established on October 31, 1981. This document defines the country and its goals. The section called "Protection of Fundamental Rights and Freedoms of the Individual" covers subjects such as protection from slavery and forced labor, meaning no person shall be held in slavery or servitude and no person shall be required to perform forced labor. Also covered is protection from inhumane treatment, meaning no person shall be subjected to torture, inhumane or degrading punishment, or other such treatment.

The constitution also establishes the different branches of the government and their purposes. It defines the regulations and restrictions

The national flag was designed by art teacher Reginald Samuel in 1966. The sun represents the dawn of a new era. The black background stands for African heritage. Red is for the blood of enslaved ancestors and the energy of the people. Blue signifies hope. The large V shape stands for victory. The colors yellow, blue, and white stand for the sun, sea, and sand.

of Parliament. The police service commission rules are laid out. In addition, the constitution states what classifies citizenship.

## THE EXECUTIVE BRANCH

The executive branch is made up of the head of state and the head of government. The British monarchy—the head of state—is hereditary. The prime minister is the head of government and the political leader of the country. He or she (as of 2021, there has not been a female prime minister of this country) is chosen through democratic elections. Citizens do not vote directly for the prime minister, per se, but rather they elect members of Parliament. The political party that wins the majority of votes then chooses the prime minister.

The prime minister selects members of their cabinet from the legislative branch. The cabinet comprises the heads of different ministries including Tourism and Investment; Finance and Corporate Governance; Foreign Affairs, Immigration and Trade; Education, Science and Technology; and others.

## THE LEGISLATIVE BRANCH

This branch is bicameral, which means it is made up of two legislative chambers, the House of Representatives and the Senate. The House has 18 members who are elected by popular vote every 5 years. The Senate has 17 members, but they are appointed by the leaders in government. The purpose of the House of Representatives is to present new legislation. The Senate then reviews and approves any proposed legislation. Following the 2018 elections and appointments, the House was made up of 16 men and 2 women; the Senate had 8 men and 9 women.

The leader of the party that holds the most seats in the House of Representatives becomes the prime minister. To ensure that the opposition is given a voice in government, the governor-general appoints an opposition leader. The leader is typically one who receives the most support from members of the legislative branch who oppose the majority government. When appointed commissions are assembled, the leader of the opposition is included along with the governor-general and the prime minister.

One of the duties of the prime minister includes appointing 11 of the 17 seats in the Senate with the approval of the governor-general. One of these members must reside in Barbuda. The opposition leader must advise appointments for four senators to the governor-general. One of the two remaining senators is appointed by the governor-general and the other on the advice of the Barbuda Council.

## THE JUDICIAL BRANCH

The magistrates of the judicial branch are appointed by the Office of the Attorney General in the executive branch. Even so, this branch remains comparatively independent of the legislative and executive branches.

This photo shows the entry hall of Government House in Saint John's. It has been the residence and office of the islands' governor-general since 1800.

*In 1834, when slavery was outlawed in British territories, the emancipated people living on Barbuda believed the island belonged to all of them, as a community. There was no private property. By custom, this communal form of land ownership was passed on through the generations without challenge, subject only to occasional disagreements between neighbors. This communal arrangement was specific only to Barbuda, not Antigua.*

*In 2007, this custom was codified (made into law) in the Barbuda Land Act. The law states, "All land in Barbuda shall be owned in common by the people of Barbuda," and, "No land in Barbuda shall be sold." The act specified that residents must consent to major development projects on the island. In 2016, the act was amended, raising the value of development projects to be subject to public approval from $5.4 million to $40 million. Developments worth less than $40 million would not need to be voted on by the citizens.*

*Prime Minister Gaston Browne, who took office in 2014, supports privatizing the land on Barbuda. The issue became urgent following Hurricane Irma in 2017, which left Barbuda so utterly demolished that it was difficult to identify some former properties, none of which had been surveyed. Browne wanted citizens to purchase their current plots of land for $1. In return, landowners would receive deeds exchangeable for bank loans to rebuild homes destroyed by the hurricane. The government's attitude is that the land in Barbuda belongs to the government, not to the Barbudans.*

*However, many in Barbuda are opposed to changing the system. They fear the island will be taken over by wealthy landowners and foreign-owned resorts, crowding out the people who have historically lived there. They have filed legal challenges, on the grounds that the government's actions are unconstitutional, and the matter remains tied up in the courts.*

The judicial branch is composed of the Magistrates' Courts, which handle minor offenses, and the High Court, which deals with major offenses. The Magistrates' Courts are the main courts for Antigua and Barbuda. They are divided into three districts. Each district has a magistrate who is also a justice of the peace. This magistrate is responsible for conducting preliminary inquiries regarding criminal charges and for settling small civil claims.

*Although the island nation can appear to be a laid-back tropical paradise, its culture is based on a history of stern Christian religious and moral traditions. Some of its laws today reflect this part of its history, and visitors are often advised to be mindful of their behavior.*

*Same-sex sexual activity is outlawed in Antigua and Barbuda, subject to a 15-year prison sentence—and same-sex marriage is likewise not recognized. Homophobic laws are not often prosecuted, but they remain on the books, and constitutional protections do not exist for LGBTQ+ people. Such individuals often face discrimination and occasionally face abuse too. LGBTQ+ tourists are advised to be discreet.*

*Laws against illegal drug use or drug trafficking are likewise very strict, resulting in long prison sentences and hefty fines.*

*In addition, there are laws against using offensive language (swearing) in public spaces, and—perhaps curiously—against the wearing of camouflage clothing.*

To go beyond these local courts, a case can be passed to the Eastern Caribbean States Supreme Court located in Saint Lucia. This court consists of the Court of Appeal and a High Court of Justice. It acts as the superior court of record for Antigua and Barbuda, British Virgin Islands, Dominica, Grenada, Montserrat, Saint Kitts and Nevis, Anguilla, Saint Lucia, and Saint Vincent and the Grenadines. All are members of the Organization of Eastern Caribbean States (OECS).

The last court of appeal is located in London, England, and is called the Judicial Committee of Privy Council. Once a decision is made by this court for any OECS member, it is final and cannot be appealed to any other court.

## THE BARBUDA COUNCIL

This council was established in 1976 and is responsible for running the internal affairs of the island of Barbuda. It consists of 11 members. Nine of these members are elected by voters of Barbuda. The other two are the Barbudan representative and senator of the legislative branch in the national government.

The purpose of the Barbuda Council is to control and oversee public health, public utilities, agriculture, forestry, and road maintenance. It also raises and collects revenue to cover its expenses.

## DEFENSE

The defense force was formed after independence. Prior to that it was a volunteer force called the Antigua Defense Force. Its main purpose was to protect the interest of the sugarcane planters. Today, the Antigua and Barbuda

A military band is shown here on November 20, 2016, celebrating the 35th anniversary of independence in Antigua and Barbuda.

Defense Force protects the civilian population of the country. Some of its duties are to prevent smuggling, provide internal security, and conduct search and rescue operations. In 2019, the defense force consisted of about 200 active personnel in two branches, the Coast Guard and the Antigua and Barbuda Regiment. Its headquarters are located near Parham at Camp Blizzard, which used to be a U.S. Navy facility.

## INTERNET LINKS

**ab.gov.ag**
This is the site for Antigua and Barbuda's Government Information and Services.

**ab.gov.ag/detail_page.php?page=27**
The complete text of the constitution of Antigua and Barbuda is available on this site.

**www.bbc.com/news/stories-49210150**
The controversy regarding Barbudan land rights is discussed in this article.

**freedomhouse.org/country/antigua-and-barbuda/freedom-world/2020**
This pro-democracy organization reports on the country's political rights and civil liberties.

**www.state.gov/reports/2018-country-reports-on-human-rights-practices/antigua-and-barbuda**
The U.S. State Department reports on human rights in Antigua and Barbuda.

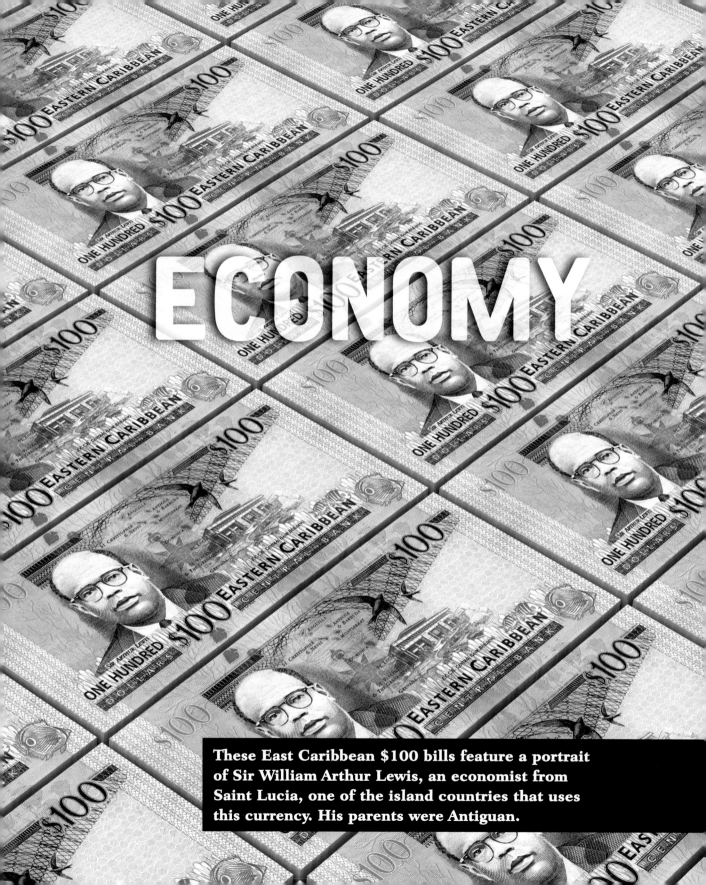

# ECONOMY

These East Caribbean $100 bills feature a portrait of Sir William Arthur Lewis, an economist from Saint Lucia, one of the island countries that uses this currency. His parents were Antiguan.

**4**

LIKE MOST CARIBBEAN ISLAND economies, Antigua's was built on sugar. As sweet as that sounds, the reality was bitter. It would be more accurate to say that Antigua was built on the blood, sweat, and misery of enslaved people over a period of more than two centuries. Sugarcane was simply the crop of choice.

European settlers arriving in the early 1600s began farming tobacco, indigo, cotton, ginger, and other crops that do well in tropical climates. However, sugarcane quickly proved to be the most profitable, and great plantations were dedicated to its production. Although Christopher Columbus first brought sugarcane to the Caribbean islands on his second voyage in 1494, it wasn't until 1650 that the first sugarcane farm was built on Antigua. Sir Christopher Codrington acquired the property in 1674, named it Betty's Hope, and built it into the island's largest sugar plantation, run by around 400 enslaved laborers. (Barbuda, for its part, was never suited to large-scale agricultural endeavors, but it did house hundreds of enslaved people who worked on Antigua.)

Sugar quickly became an important leg of the "triangle trade" between Europe, Africa, and the Americas. People were captured in Africa and sold to plantation owners in the Caribbean. There, they grew sugarcane and made it into sugar, molasses, and rum. These products were then sold to the American colonies and Europe. The European ships would then

An economy is the complex set of interrelated activities that involve the making (creating, building, growing); distributing (selling); and consumption (buying, using, eating, saving) of goods and services in a particular place. National economies are typically categorized into three parts, or sectors: agriculture (farming, logging and fishing), industry (manufacturing and mining), and service. In the last century, Antigua's economy has shifted from an agricultural to a service economy.

*Gross domestic product (GDP) is a measure of a country's total production. The number reflects the total value of goods and services produced over one year. Economists use it to determine whether a country's economy is growing or contracting. Growth is good, while a falling GDP means trouble. Dividing the GDP by the number of people in the country determines the GDP per capita (per person). This number provides an indication of a country's average standard of living—the higher the better.*

*In 2019, the GDP per capita (adjusted to purchasing power parity) in Antigua and Barbuda was approximately $21,910. That figure ranked Antigua and Barbuda at 87th out of 228 countries listed by the CIA World Factbook. For comparison, the United States that year was number 15, with a GDP per capita of $62,530. Neighboring islands in the Caribbean's Lesser Antilles fared similarly—with the U.S. Virgin Islands ranking 54th, with a GDP per capita of $37,000, and Dominica coming in on the lower end at number 133, with a GDP per capita of $11,917.*

return to Africa with guns, gunpowder, and other cargo to trade for people to enslave. Then, the triangular cycle of trade would repeat.

After Britain outlawed the slave trade in 1833, plantation owners began importing indentured servants from South Asia to take the place of enslaved Africans. These Asian workers toiled under conditions similar to slavery, alongside some emancipated Africans who continued to work the plantations for extremely low wages. Despite these adaptations to changing times, the sugar plantations of Antigua were unable to compete with larger sugar industries in Brazil and elsewhere. In addition, the long-term cultivation of sugarcane had seriously damaged the island's environment, with the destruction of forests, pollution of water, and erosion and depletion of soil. By the mid-20th century, the cane plantations and mills were all but out of business.

Today, sugar is mostly a bittersweet memory on Antigua. Betty's Hope no longer functions as a plantation or sugar mill. It has been partly restored as a historical open-air museum. However, sugarcane remains the world's largest single commercial crop. In 2019—2020, Brazil was the largest sugar producer, with India coming in a close second.

Antigua's economic foundation has shifted from sugar to hospitality. Tourism now accounts for about 60 percent of the island nation's GDP.

## TOURISM

Antigua's famed 365 beaches, turquoise waters, and pleasant climate are a strong attraction to winter-weary North Americans and Europeans. In 2019, Antigua and Barbuda's tourism sector was booming. That year, the country welcomed 300,000 visitors, a new milestone. New luxury resorts were opening, and the main seaport in Saint John's was getting a major makeover.

Peak tourist season runs from mid-December to mid-April. In January, the average temperature is a very comfortable 76°F (24.5°C). Summertime finds Antigua less crowded, as the temperature is warmer, though not unbearable. June is the hottest month, with an average temperature of 82°F (28°C). June through November is hurricane season, and September to November is the rainy season; therefore prices tend to be lower.

A woman peruses the souvenir offerings at a colorful market in Long Bay Beach, Antigua.

*Typically, countries with larger service sectors are considered more advanced than industrial or agricultural economies. The service sector includes a broad range of economic activities that do not, themselves, produce specific goods. Rather, these businesses offer services (hence the name), from house cleaning to ballet lessons to brain surgery. People who make cars, for example, are in the manufacturing sector, but people who fix those cars are in the service sector. The service industry includes legal services; architectural, engineering, and construction companies; accounting and advertising firms; telecommunications enterprises; the arts, entertainment, and recreation industries; social services such as health care and education; wholesaling, retailing, and franchising businesses; railway and trucking firms; utility companies; and—most relevant in the case of Antigua and*

Tourists shop on St. Mary's Street in Saint John's.

*Barbuda—travel and tourism services. These include hotels, restaurants, car rentals, and many other businesses that directly or indirectly cater to tourists.*

Vacationers fly to the islands or arrive on cruise ships. They snorkel in the crystal clear waters, explore pristine beaches, or shop in Saint John's. The towns of Falmouth Harbour, English Harbour, and Jolly Harbour are other popular tourist destinations. Huge yachts dock in these harbors, which are set up like small towns with facilities for fresh water, electricity, diesel fuel, restaurants, and shops. Cruise ships deliver an additional 788,000 money-spending day-trippers each year. Visitors from the United States account for about one-third of all tourist arrivals in Antigua and Barbuda.

However, having a tourism-based economy leaves the island nation vulnerable in a number of ways. Tourism can be strongly impacted by both natural and human-made disasters. In recent years, Antigua has suffered catastrophes of both sorts, which have sent the economy reeling.

**CRIME AND CORRUPTION**    At the end of the 20th century, a succession of high-level corruption, money-laundering, and online-gambling scandals—some linked to the prime minister and his family—hurt the country's reputation. In 1999, the U.S. State Department reported that the country was "one of the most attractive centers in the Caribbean for money launderers." In 2008, the highly publicized murder of a British couple honeymooning in Antigua—a crime committed by two local men in what appeared to be a random robbery gone wrong—cast a shadow over tourist safety. In 2009, the island's largest private investor, an American named Allen Stanford, was arrested for running a massive, fraudulent financial scheme out of Antigua, deeply shaking the country's financial foundation. The 2009 global economic crisis further hurt the island nation. All of this led to a steep decline in tourism that lasted through around 2011.

**NATURAL DISASTERS**    The devastation caused by Hurricane Irma and the other 2017 hurricanes deeply impacted the islands' tourism industry. Barbuda was completely shut down, with virtually all of its homes, hotels, and restaurants destroyed. Those were not the first hurricanes to cause significant damage to the islands; in 1995, Hurricane Luis hit both Barbuda and Antigua, demolishing 70 percent of houses on Barbuda and 45 percent of

Money laundering is the process of disguising or hiding the origins of illegally obtained money. This may include the profits from drug trafficking, the financing of terrorist activities, tax evasion, or some other criminal activity. Money laundering is typically done through a scheme of complex transactions, often involving foreign banks or the establishment of fake businesses (shell companies), with the goal of making large amounts of money appear to have come from legitimate sources.

# THE COVID-19 PANDEMIC

*Antigua and Barbuda was only just beginning to recover from the onslaught of the 2017 hurricane season when a completely new sort of problem hit. The COVID-19 global pandemic was a combination human–natural disaster, and it posed an enormous threat to the islands' economy. In the late winter of 2020, tourism around the world came screeching to a halt as foreign travelers everywhere clamored to get home. The first appearance of the illness in Antigua and Barbuda was noted on March 10, 2020. On March 27, the government instituted a state of emergency and closed the borders of Antigua and Barbuda to incoming yachts.*

*The country remained closed until June 1. During that time, mandatory mask-wearing regulations went into effect and strict limitations were placed on public gatherings. Hand-washing sinks were installed outside shops, and an old hospital ward was converted into a new infectious diseases center in Saint John's, specifically for COVID-19 patients. The country also created a robust track-and-trace system to follow the spread of the disease.*

*When Antigua and Barbuda reopened in June 2020, incoming visitors at the V. C. Bird International Airport were met by officials in full PPE (personal protective equipment) and were required to present a negative COVID-19 test result, taken within the previous seven days. The island nation had to make further adjustments when Canada, the United States, and the United Kingdom began requiring negative COVID-19 tests for people returning home from a visit to the islands. In January 2021, the Ministry of Health, Wellness and the Environment approved on-site rapid antigen testing services to guests.*

*The stringent measures were largely successful. In March 2021, the island nation reported a total of 1,080 cases, 715 recoveries, and 28 deaths from the virus. However, the economy of the islands suffered greatly.*

*"COVID has been extremely devastating to our economy," Prime Minister Gaston Browne told news sources in November 2020. "We're one of the most tourism-dependent countries in the world and, as a consequence, our revenues fell by as much as 60 percent at one point. A lot of people were put out of work as a result of closure of the tourism sector, as airlines and cruise ships discontinued service."*

those on Antigua, along with power outages and disrupted water systems. Hurricane Luis ultimately caused three deaths and 165 injuries and left around 3,000 people homeless. In 1999, Hurricane Jose caused massive flooding on Antigua, 1 death, and 12 injuries, along with tremendous damage.

Hurricane season is one reason why tourism drops in the late summer and early autumn, as the fierce Atlantic storms are an ongoing threat. However, the destruction of Barbuda in 2017 was unprecedented.

## AGRICULTURE

Agriculture was once the foundation of Antigua and Barbuda's economy, but in 2017 it made up only 1.8 percent of the GDP. As agriculture has fallen into general decline across the islands, the people must rely heavily on imported foodstuffs. Most of the island farms are small, dedicated to growing fruits and vegetables only for local consumption. One exception to this is the production of sea-island cotton, a crop that is prized for its long, silky fibers. The reintroduction of this rare cotton as a commercial product in Antigua is a recent endeavor, with most of the crop so far being exported to Japan.

Antigua's famous black pineapples grow on a plantation on the island.

A wide variety of crops grow in Antigua and Barbuda's tropical climate. Most of Antigua's usable agricultural land lies in the southern part of the island. There, farmers grow cucumbers, coconuts, mangoes, melons, pumpkins, limes, Antiguan black pineapples, and sweet potatoes. Antigua's most important root crop is the sweet potato. It is included in many Antiguan recipes. People living on Barbuda have small personal plots of land, where they grow peanuts, corn, melons, and coconuts.

Other fruits and vegetables include passionfruit, bananas, cantaloupes, papayas, avocados, and cherries. Fruits grow in abundance in the wild, and dates and sea grapes can be found hanging from trees and bushes. Other vegetables include carrots, cabbage, squash, and a variety of peppers.

Even though wild sugarcane can be found throughout the island, very little is cultivated as a crop. However, some industrious vendors will chop the canes down, peel off the thick bark, and chop the cane into small pieces. These are then put into a plastic bag and sold along the road or in the markets.

**WATER**   Agriculture on Antigua and Barbuda has one major obstacle—an insufficient supply of fresh water. The islands have no permanent, year-round rivers. Several recent years of prolonged drought exacerbated the problem, and islanders have been forced to ration water. To supplement reliance on rainfall, the government has installed three desalination plants on the coast of Antigua.

**LIVESTOCK**   Individual homeowners and small farmers keep cattle, pigs, goats, and sheep. It's not uncommon to see herds of goats and sheep wandering along the roads in the countryside. Drivers must be especially careful not to hit them while coming around sharp curves.

It can be difficult to tell the goats and sheep apart, since the sheep on Antigua do not have thick wool. There is a local saying that "goat's tails are up and sheep tails are down."

On Barbuda, there are many wild donkeys. These feral animals are descendants of tame donkeys that were introduced by Europeans in the 15th century. They were used for transportation for centuries but have long since been replaced by cars and bicycles. Once these new forms of transport arrived in Barbuda, the donkeys were left to fend for themselves. Today, thousands of wild donkeys roam the island in herds.

**FISHERIES**   Crab, shrimp, and lobster farming also falls under the heading of agriculture, and there are farming operations for all three of those shellfish on the islands. However, success in aquaculture has been limited. Seaweed farming has achieved some success in Antigua but is still very small in scale.

Most fishing is also small scale and for local consumption—the people of Antigua and Barbuda are great lovers of seafood. Antiguans annually consume more fish per capita (101.4 pounds/46 kilograms) per year than any other nation or territory in the Caribbean.

The fishing industry has been hard hit several times—particularly in 2017—by hurricanes destroying fleets of fishing boats.

Fishing boats are a colorful sight in the harbor at Saint John's.

## MANUFACTURING

Industry contributes about 20.8 percent to the nation's GDP. This includes construction, which is tied to the building of new tourist resorts, as well as to rebuilding after natural disasters. Light manufacturing plays a small role, producing clothing, paints, furniture, food, and beverages. Assembly lines that put together electrical components and household appliances can also be found in Antigua. Many of these factories are located on Factory Road, close to the international airport. In addition, Individual artisans on the islands produce handicrafts for the tourist market.

## BANKING AND FINANCIAL SERVICES

Money is an important business for the island nation. The financial service industry is dominated by both domestic and international banks, insurance companies, and other financial organizations. Antigua and Barbuda has the second-largest banking sector in the Eastern Caribbean, accounting for about 20 percent of the region's deposits, loans, and assets. In the past, Antigua and Barbuda was accused of having weak anti—money laundering laws, prompting sanctions from the United Kingdom and the United States. The country has since tightened its laws to the satisfaction of most foreign countries.

## TRANSPORTATION

Antigua and Barbuda has a total of 240 miles (386 km) of paved roads and 487 miles (784 km) of unpaved roads. Getting around Antigua is relatively easy. Tourist buses speed along the roads, taking cruise ship passengers on day excursions, such as diving with the rays. Service vehicles, such as heavy construction trucks and phone repair vehicles, are also able to maneuver around the island easily. Traffic can get quite heavy in Saint John's during rush hour, but it lightens up closer to the outer villages.

Occasionally, a man may be spotted riding a mule, or boys can be seen riding horses along the road. Even though this form of transportation is not common, it still exists.

On the island of Barbuda, there are no paved roads. All of the roads are made of dirt, gravel, or crushed coral. It is not uncommon to see Barbudans driving vehicles with four-wheel drive to navigate its rough road system.

Tourists arrive in Antigua at the only international airport, which is located several miles outside of Saint John's, called the V. C. Bird International Airport. Several major airlines fly to Antigua from Europe, Canada, the United States, and the Caribbean. A smaller airport is located in Barbuda. Tourists may also arrive on cruise ships, which usually dock near Redcliffe Quay and Heritage Quay in Saint John's. Cargo ships dock in Deepwater Harbour, farther away from Saint John's, next to a dockyard filled with cargo containers.

## INTERNET LINKS

**www.cia.gov/the-world-factbook/countries/antigua-and-barbuda/#economy**
The CIA *World Factbook* has up-to-date economic statistics for Antigua and Barbuda.

**www.fao.org/fishery/facp/ATG/en**
This report provides statistics on the islands' fishery operations.

**www.worldatlas.com/articles/what-are-the-biggest-industries-in-antigua-and-barbuda.html**
This page provides a quick overview of the country's economy.

# ENVIRONMENT

Cactus plants grow on a sandy beach
in Two Foot Bay, Barbuda.

# 5

ANTIGUA AND BARBUDA IS ONE OF the smallest countries in the world, with two main islands and a number of uninhabited small islands and cays. In all, it encompasses a mere 170 square miles (442 sq km). The landscape is characterized by low-lying coral and limestone formations, much of it covered with cactus scrub.

Once heavily forested, the land was long ago cleared for sugar plantations. Because of that, the region's biodiversity is not as robust as it once was. Large areas of wildlife habitat have disappeared from the overexploitation of reefs, pollution, overgrazing, and the introduction of nonindigenous species. Other causes of biodiversity destruction include drought, hurricanes, and overuse of pesticides.

The country's economy is based largely on tourism, which depends greatly on the quality of the environment. The islands, therefore, are financially motivated to manage and protect the beauty, health, and biodiversity of their natural settings. On the other hand, tourism adds a burden to the already fragile environment of the small islands.

Today, the biggest environmental concerns in Antigua and Barbuda are water management, deforestation, and the protection of native species and natural ecosystems. Densely populated areas, primarily Saint John's, also have waste-disposal problems, with open sewage causing pollution. In addition, global warming is causing climate change that threatens the islands with an increase in extreme weather events and rising sea levels.

Found only on Great Bird Island off the coast of Antigua, the harmless snake called the Antiguan racer was once one of the rarest snakes in the world. It was twice declared extinct, inaccurately, having fallen prey to rats and mongooses brought in by Europeans. Conservation efforts ridding the island of rats and mongooses in recent years have boosted numbers from an estimated 50 to more than 1,100 snakes.

Colorful fish and starfish go about their underwater lives on a coral reef off Antigua.

The country's government has demonstrated a commitment to solving these environmental issues and has made much progress. However, the financial cost of addressing these concerns is a great strain to the nation's economy, and the necessary transition to a "green economy"—an environmentally sustainable economy based on clean, renewable sources of energy—remains a challenge.

## WATER, WATER, EVERYWHERE

Although it is surrounded by water, Antigua and Barbuda has an insufficient supply of fresh water. Neither island has permanent rivers, streams, or lakes. The rainy season is short, and during years of prolonged drought, the islanders

# SAVING THE HAWKSBILL TURTLES

The indigenous hawksbill turtle is the national creature of the sea for Antigua. It was once hunted for its beautiful tortoiseshell, which is about 3 feet (0.91 m) long and weighs about 175 pounds (80 kg). These shells were used to make combs, frames for glasses, decorative fans, and cigarette boxes, but today the animals are protected. They can live up to 50 years. Hawksbill turtles do not migrate regularly like some turtles, but appear to stay in the same place. They can be found while snorkeling around the coral reefs. Antigua boasts the largest nesting area of hawksbills in the Caribbean, with about 500 hawksbill nests and around 18,000 hatchlings produced in a year. (Most hatchlings do not survive.)

The hawksbill reached endangered status through a loss of nesting and feeding habitats, pollution, egg-collection, and development on coastlines. Even though they are now protected, these turtles are still poached and killed for their shells.

The Jumby Bay Hawksbill Project began in 1986. Today, its biologists continuously patrol the nesting beaches between June and November. They look for tracks made in the sand by female hawksbills that have come ashore to lay their eggs. Once the female begins laying her eggs, she goes into a sort of trancelike state. During this time, the biologists can do a number of tests, which they document. These tests include measuring her shell, counting how many eggs she has laid, and giving her an identification tag. If she already has a tag, it is noted. All of this data tracks the turtle population.

This project is very important for this critically endangered species. Antigua and Barbuda is also home to important populations of leatherback and green turtles. It's illegal to harvest all species of marine turtles from the islands' waters, and it is also illegal to poach the eggs or disturb nesting females.

have been forced to ration water. Agricultural and industrial development has strained the water supply and sometimes pollutes what is there.

To lessen reliance on rainfall, the government installed three desalination plants on the coast of Antigua, thus creating a continuous supply of water from the Caribbean Sea. Barbuda also has a desalination plant in addition to wells, some of which were dug during the time of Christopher Codrington. The public water supply for Barbuda is supplied from a single well that serves the town of Codrington, where most of the population lives. Throughout the island, the groundwater is generally saline (salt water), with the notable exception of Palmetto Sands on the southwestern shore.

Said to be the world's sweetest pineapple, Antigua black pineapples are displayed at a fruit and vegetable market in Saint John's.

# NATIONAL PARKS, PROTECTED AREAS, AND NATURAL REFUGES

Indigenous animals have suffered from the influx of alien species over the centuries. Individual Antiguans, with government support, have made a huge effort to maintain the natural wonders that exist in this island country. The creation of protected areas has helped tremendously in this regard.

One such natural refuge for a variety of endangered species is Great Bird Island. This very small island is about 1.9 miles (3 km) northeast of Antigua. Sailors named it Great Bird Island years ago because of the huge amount of birds they found living there. Endangered species found there are brown pelicans, West Indian whistling ducks, red-billed tropicbirds, and a rare lizard. It is also the only place in the world where you can see the Antiguan racer snake in the wild.

The indigenous Antiguan racer was almost lost as a species to the appetites of imported rats and mongooses.

A colony of magnificent frigate birds roost in mangrove trees in the Frigate Bird Sanctuary in Codrington Lagoon.

**FRIGATE BIRD SANCTUARY** Codrington Lagoon on Barbuda is where the national bird of Antigua, the frigate bird, lives in a protected sanctuary. There are five species of frigate birds worldwide. Two of these species are endangered. However, the one found on Barbuda, the magnificent frigate bird, is not. Even so, it is important to protect these huge birds. Codrington Lagoon is home to the largest nesting colony of frigate birds in the world. It is also one of the world's most important areas for preserving these birds as there are few predators in this area. Thousands of frigate birds breed and nest there from September to April. Even though there are many frigate birds in one place, they are amazingly quiet, making only soft twittering noises.

Both male and female birds are shiny and black. The main difference between the two is that the female has a white breast and the male has a bright red breast. During mating, to attract a female, the male expands his red breast like a balloon and thumps it with his beak, making a soft drumming noise. The female lays only one egg in a nest built on mangrove trees. Once hatched, the baby chicks are covered in white down, much like a cotton ball. The chick depends on its parents for up to 11 months before it can fend for itself.

The wings on these large birds are a little over 7 feet (2.1 m) long from tip to tip, and they weigh about 3 pounds (1.4 kg) each. Their diet consists mostly of fish that they often steal from other birds.

These huge birds glide with the air currents. Like most birds, frigate birds are excellent at flying. However, they swim and walk with much difficulty because of their weak legs. If a frigate accidentally lands in the water, scientists have observed other frigates coming to the drowning bird's rescue and pulling it safely to shore.

**WALLINGS FOREST AND RESERVOIR**    On the southwest side of Antigua is Wallings Forest and Reservoir. Originally, Wallings was a water reservoir designed to hold millions of gallons of water. Because the area was used as a reservoir, its forests were completely stripped by 1900. In 1915, tree seeds were planted on a 13-acre (5.5 hectare) section of Wallings to reforest the area. Some of the trees that can be found at Wallings today are locusts, ironwoods, mahoes, mangoes, white cedars, mahoganies, and Spanish oaks.

In the 1990s, Wallings Forest and Reservoir was established as a conservation area. This was done by Antigua and Barbuda's government with the assistance of the Island Resources Foundation.

**DEVIL'S BRIDGE PARK**    In the 1950s, the northeastern point of Antigua was officially made a national park. It is known as Devil's Bridge Park

Devil's Bridge is a natural formation on the Atlantic Ocean side of Antigua.

because of the natural arch found there, which has been carved by years of seawater erosion. This limestone bridge is about 30 feet (9 m) long and 12 feet (3.6 m) high.

## ENVIRONMENTAL ORGANIZATIONS

Environmental education has become a useful tool in preserving the islands' natural wonders. The Environmental Awareness Group of Antigua and Barbuda is the leading nongovernmental organization; it sponsors educational projects and programs for adults and kids. The group runs the Offshore Islands Conservation Program to help protect the indigenous flora and fauna of the offshore islands. It also sponsors turtle and seabird protection programs. The organization helped to advocate for a ban on single-use plastic bags, which went into effect in Antigua and Barbuda in 2016.

The Antigua Conservation Society is another active nonprofit. It is focused on coastal and marine ecosystems. In 2019, the island country joined the United Nations' (UN's) Clean Seas campaign, the world's largest alliance for combating marine plastic pollution.

## INTERNET LINKS

**www.fauna-flora.org/species/antiguan-racer**
Discussion of the Antiguan racer is presented on this site.

**www.jbhp.org**
The Jumby Bay Hawksbill Project has information about the turtles and conservation efforts.

**www.nationalparksantigua.com**
This site provides information on the various ecosystems and environmental threats on the islands.

**www.worldwildlife.org/ecoregions/nt0220**
This site provides information on the ecology of the Lesser Antilles islands region.

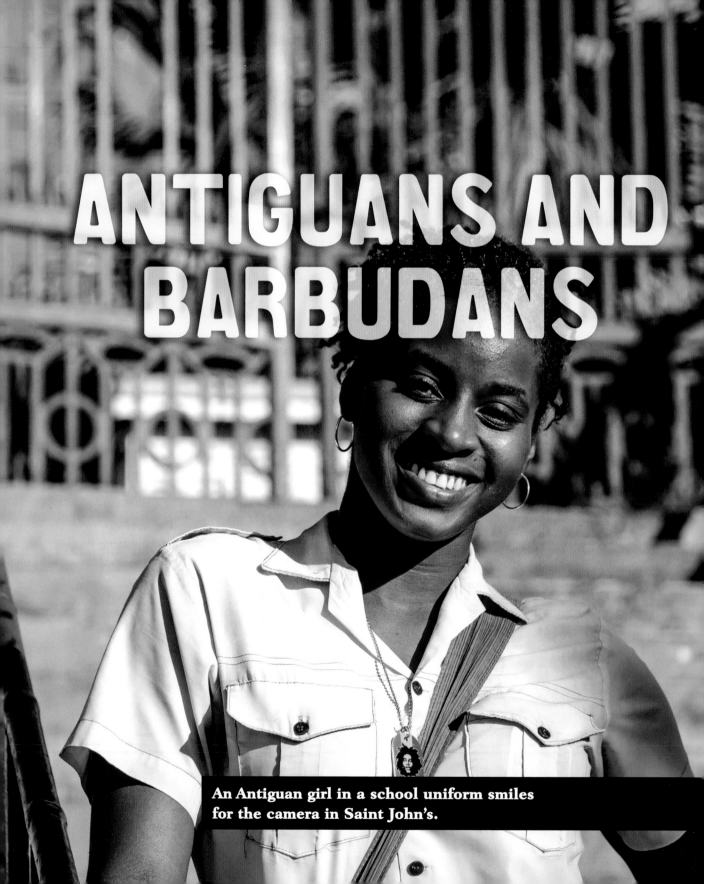

# ANTIGUANS AND BARBUDANS

An Antiguan girl in a school uniform smiles for the camera in Saint John's.

**6**

D EPENDING ON WHICH OF THE TWO islands they live on, the people of this Caribbean nation are Antiguans or Barbudans. By far, most people live on Antigua—around 97 percent of the population—and the small number of Barbudans live mostly in the island's one town of Codrington. Antiguans and Barbudans are overwhelmingly of Black African ancestry, the descendants of the thousands of enslaved people brought to these islands centuries ago to work on the plantations. Nearly from the very beginning of European occupation of the islands, the enslaved people outnumbered the white colonizers.

Over time, migrants from other parts of the world arrived. After the slave trade was outlawed, indentured servants from South Asia were brought to the islands to work, and many never returned home. Portuguese workers arrived in the 19th century, fleeing a famine. Itinerant traders from the Middle East arrived around the turn of the 20th century. Though they were from various countries, they tended to be called Syrians.

Census results have reported about 87 percent of the Antiguan and Barbudan people to be of Black African descent. Mixed-race people made up 4.7 percent; Hispanic people accounted for about 2.7 percent; and white people (mostly of British descent) made up 1.6 percent of the population. The remaining 2.7 percent "other" and 0.9 percent "unspecified" were South Asian, Middle Eastern, Amerindian, or Chinese.

Spectators at a parade celebrating the beginning of Carnival in Saint John's are ready for fun.

More recently, Spanish-speaking people from other Caribbean islands and South America have arrived. Also, about 4,500 people living in Antigua and Barbuda are from the United States.

## FROM AFRICANS TO ANTIGUANS

The bonds of slavery were never accepted by the captive Africans. There are accounts of runaways starting in 1680. Enslaved Africans began organizing revolts against their white masters as early as 1687. Stories of runaway camps established on Boggy Peak, rewards for captured runaways, and occasional revolts continued through the late 17th and early 18th centuries. The largest planned rebellion recorded was in 1736.

Three enslaved people formulated a plan in a ravine or gully called Stony Hill Gully. Their names were Prince Klaas, Tomboy, and Hercules. Their plan was to invade a ball held in honor of King George II's coronation at Christopher Dunbar's house in Saint John's. The majority of plantation owners were going to attend. Three groups of 350 enslaved people were to enter Saint John's during the ball and kill all the white people. The uprising was never executed, as the ball was postponed and an enslaved man named Johnny told the authorities about the plan. The three ringleaders were executed at the market. In addition, many other enslaved people were put to death.

Enslaved people on Barbuda had a bit more independence because they could farm their own plots of land and worked as herdsmen, hunters, and fishermen. They were also taught to become craftsmen, working as tanners, shoemakers, and carpenters. Even though their situation was considered less miserable than that of their counterparts on Antigua, there was still much anger and dissatisfaction because of their enslavement.

The first uprising of enslaved people on Barbuda was recorded in 1741 and was initiated because of a cruel manager. The enslaved people killed several cows and damaged equipment. Several uprisings occurred throughout the years, but the most serious one was between 1834 and 1835. All Barbudans were told that they were to be shipped to Antigua to work on Codrington's plantations. This caused intense anger. Troops had to be sent from Antigua to stop the revolt. Another issue that instigated this revolt was the British Parliament's failure to name Barbudans in the Slavery Emancipation Act of 1833. Instead, Barbudans had to take steps to free themselves.

Even though slavery was abolished in 1834, many former enslaved people continued working for plantation owners under very similar circumstances, for very meager salaries.

## ON BARBUDA

Additional developments continued that began to form the current country of Antigua and Barbuda as it is today. In 1860, the British Parliament made Barbuda a dependency of Antigua. Even so, the government of Antigua did not set up an administration for Barbuda because it was still leased to the Codringtons. By 1870, the Black Barbudans began complaining of their treatment on the island. The governor of Antigua canceled the Codringtons' lease to Barbuda,

A man on a paddleboard glides over a sunken shipwreck off the coast of Antigua and Barbuda.

which ended their long association with the island.

Disputes between the Antiguan government and the black Barbudans about property ownership began in 1904. Barbudans considered all land to be communal property, whereas the government wanted them to pay rent. Overall, Barbudans ignored any demands for rent payment.

In 1915, a struggle with the Antiguan government took place. A shipwreck was found off the coast of Barbuda, and the locals began to salvage its cargo and equipment. A warden of the Antiguan government arrived, demanding 10 percent of the salvage. Barbudans believed that when the Codringtons left the island, they had also left the Barbudans the right to all salvage. The Barbudans burned the warden's boat and cart in response to his demands. The governor of Antigua threatened to enforce rent payments if the culprits were not found. In the end, the matter was left unresolved.

## LABOR CONDITIONS

In contrast, by 1918, freed Black Antiguans were becoming more educated and started understanding their rights. The Black workers on Antigua began demanding an honest pay for their work. It was widely known that the local planters were getting high prices for their crops, but the profits were not passed on. These same planters still paid the Black workers very low wages.

Tempers flared, and a riot followed. Dissatisfied workers threw rocks at the police and defense force. Shots were fired back. By the end of the riot, two people were dead and 13 had been injured. The riot, however, proved fruitless as there was no rise in wages for Black Antiguans. Many became homeless and were beggars.

*Born on the outskirts of Saint John's on December 9, 1909, Vere Cornwall (V. C.) Bird was raised in abject poverty. His parents were Barbara Edghill and Theophilus Bird, and Vere was the fourth of their five children. He attended Saint John's Boys' School where he received an elementary school education.*

*When he was older, he joined the Salvation Army and was sent to Jamaica to receive training. While there, he visited many other Caribbean islands. He was deeply touched by the extreme poverty he witnessed in the area and decided to make it his life's mission to change this.*

*In 1939, V. C. Bird was selected to attend a meeting in Antigua and Barbuda. Sir Walter Citrine, a member of the Royal Commission, called the meeting. He was sent to the area to investigate what was causing the workers' riots. The outcome of this meeting was the formation of the Antigua Trades and Labour Union. Bird became an executive member of the newly established union. By 1943, he had become the union's president.*

*After the labor union was created, it immediately won several victories that began establishing workers' rights. Even though there was progress, the political power of Antigua was still held by the plantation owners. The members of the labor union soon realized that in order to gain control for the workers, the union would have to hold political power. As a result, the Antigua Labour Party (ALP) was established in 1946. Bird was encouraged to run for election to become a member of the Legislative Council, which he won in 1946.*

*As Antigua began to gain more independence from Great Britain, Bird was appointed as the first chief minister of Antigua and Barbuda in 1960. This position helped Bird shape the political structure of the country. He was chosen to be the first prime minister of Antigua and Barbuda in 1981 after it achieved complete independence. In all, he served as prime minister of Antigua and Barbuda in two non-consecutive terms for 13 years.*

*In 1994, V. C. Bird was made a Knight of the Order of the National Hero, and he was thereafter referred to as Sir Vere Bird. He was the country's first national hero. After a prolonged illness, he passed away on June 28, 1999, at the age of 89.*

Prince Harry of the United Kingdom attended a youth sports festival at Sir Vivian Richards Stadium, showcasing Antigua and Barbuda's national sports, on the second day of his official visit to the Caribbean on November 21, 2016.

Labor conditions were extremely poor until the founding of the Antigua Trades and Labour Union in 1939. This labor union was established to ensure that workers' rights would be protected. In addition, the union became a bargaining organization between plantation owners and workers. Black Antiguan workers wasted no time in joining the new union.

## AFRICAN INFLUENCES

Many customs from West Africa were handed down from generation to generation. These influences have enriched the music, arts, language, cuisine, and spiritual beliefs of the islands.

One such custom is the art of healing from wild plants, also known as bush plant healing. It began during the time of slavery. Because the enslaved people had little access to doctors, they experimented with the local plants and herbs to cure illnesses and heal the sick. This type of alternative medicine is still practiced today by the older generation but is often not being passed on to the younger generation due to a lack of interest.

Many foods were brought to Antigua and Barbuda by the African people. Some African foods include bonavista beans, okra, and eggplants. Popular African dishes are *fungee*, seasoned rice, goat water, and black pudding, a type of sausage made with cooked rice that is mixed with animal blood and seasoning; it is then stuffed into a pig or cow gut and cooked until tender.

The majority of the population in Antigua and Barbuda is Christian. However, African spiritual beliefs and superstitions have also carried down through the ages. Obeah was a form of sorcery brought from West Africa. This hard-to-define animistic belief system invokes spiritual beings—for example *jumbies,* which are mischievous spirits that live in the wild or in graveyards. Preparing herbal potions is another important part of Obeah, as well as making doll images of a person for the purpose of casting spells. For the most part, this sort of sorcery was more common in other areas of the Caribbean but is still practiced in Antigua by people who came from other countries, such as Haiti, Guadeloupe, and Dominica.

## INTERNET LINKS

**www.nytimes.com/1999/06/30/world/vere-bird-89-who-led-antigua-to-freedom.html**
The obituary for V. C. Bird provides a good overview of his life and contributions.

**www.worldatlas.com/articles/what-is-the-ethnic-composition-of-antigua-and-barbuda.html**
Basic ethnic population statistics are provided on this site.

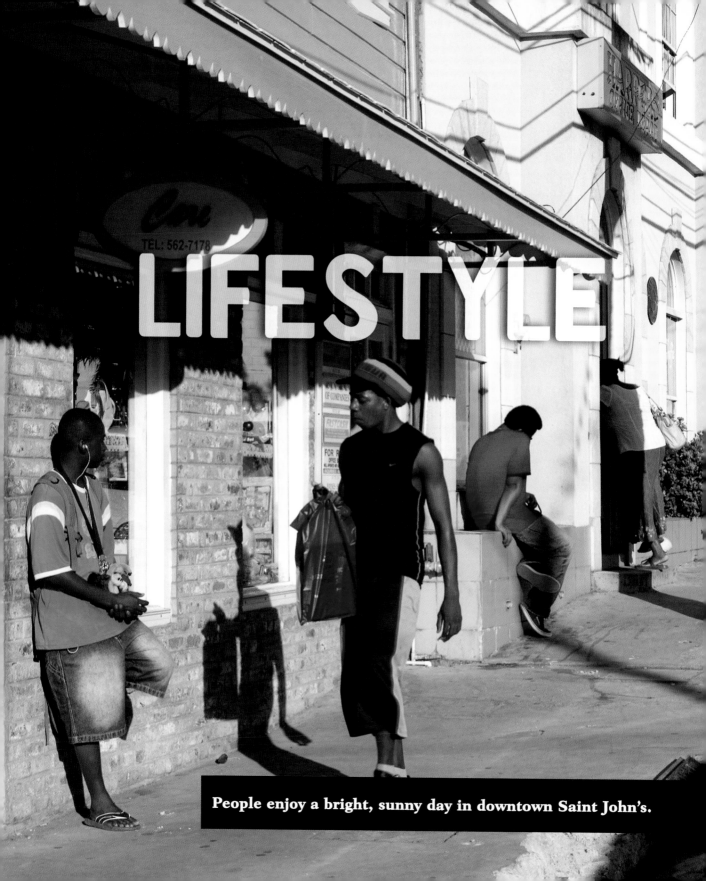

LIFESTYLE

People enjoy a bright, sunny day in downtown Saint John's.

# 7

THE CARIBBEAN LIFESTYLE IS famously laid-back and easygoing. For visitors to the islands, the slow pace of life is an escape from the frenzy of their everyday existence. For the people of Antigua and Barbuda, however, life is not an escape, and the beautiful setting is not always paradise. Work still has to be done.

However, there is an aspect to island life that fits the stereotype. Most people live in small villages where everyone knows each other's business. On Barbuda, it is thought that everyone is somehow related. Time moves slowly as people congregate on their porches or on the street to visit, have a barbecue, or play a game of cards. Wandering domesticated animals are also part of village life. Roosters scratch dirt, while goats and sheep bleat and wander from place to place.

## CLOTHING

People in Antigua and Barbuda wear Western-style clothing appropriate for tropical weather. Men usually wear blue jeans, shorts, or cotton slacks with T-shirts or button-down shirts. Baseball caps are sometimes worn to shade them from the sun.

Women wear dresses or skirts with loose-fitting tops. They also wear cotton cropped pants and blue jeans. Businessmen and women working in offices might wear Western business suits.

Barbuda resident Edith Griffin looks at her newly reroofed home in Codrington, Barbuda, in July 2018. She had been living in a tent with her family for nine months until her Codrington home, which was ravaged by Hurricane Irma in September 2017, was finally repaired.

One tradition that has lasted from the days of slavery is women using head scarves. These ties are usually colorful and are wrapped around the head. This tradition can be traced back to Antigua and Barbuda's African roots.

During festivals, elaborate and colorful costumes are the norm. Women sometimes wear tall headdresses and ornaments attached to their backs.

Children attending school wear uniforms. Each school has a different uniform. Girls might wear skirts with blouses or dresses with a white and blue checkered pattern. Boys wear slacks or shorts with matching shirts, such as a pair of black pants with a white shirt. When boys graduate to secondary school, they have to wear a tie. All school uniforms are manufactured in Antigua.

## HOMES

The majority of houses in Antigua and Barbuda are constructed out of concrete or wood. However, some are built using the local green limestone. Most have two bedrooms, a living room, a kitchen, and a bathroom; even so, some homes are very small and often consist of only one room that is 6 feet (1.83 m) by 10 feet (3.05 m). The majority of people have indoor plumbing as well as electricity.

Houses are often painted in bright, cheerful colors, such as pink, yellow, or peach and white. Some houses are multicolored with red roofs, yellow siding, purple windows, and blue trim. Even local churches are colorful; examples are a peach-colored Catholic church and a yellow Baptist church.

## FAMILY LIFE

Couples are typically united in one of three different ways: they may be legally married; they may be unmarried but live together as family; or they may be joined in a union in which the man and woman have children together but live in different locations—this is called a visiting union. Female-headed households are widespread, and it's not uncommon for a man in Antigua or Barbuda to have two or three families living in different locations. This custom may stem from the time of slavery, in which families were routinely and callously broken up, with partners and children being sold away to others. Indeed, many laws from that era worked to undermine the family unit of enslaved people. Also, the custom may be based on present or historical economic expediency. Poverty and job opportunities may necessitate family members living apart.

The common law in Antigua and Barbuda identifies that children should receive care and attention by their parents. However, because of economic or other factors, children may or may not be raised by their parents; instead, they may be raised in a variety of households or with relatives.

Under Antiguan and Barbudan law, there is no difference between the children born in or out of wedlock. In 1987, a law called the Status of Children Act was passed, making it illegal to discriminate against children born to unwed parents, especially concerning inheritance. In addition, the father of the child, whether married to the mother or not, is responsible for paying child support.

## THE ROLE OF WOMEN

Antigua and Barbuda is committed to advancing gender equality, though there is still room for improvement. Women on this twin-island country have access

*The best way to assess a nation's general health is by examining certain statistical indicators and comparing them to those of other countries. One of the primary measures used is life expectancy at birth. This figure is the average number of years a person born in a certain year can expect to live, if mortality factors remain constant. (However, these factors don't remain constant over time, so this statistic is hypothetical.) Since this figure is an average of all life spans within a given framework, it cannot predict any specific person's length of life.*

*Life expectancy at birth is used to compare conditions in different countries, but it also reflects trends up or down within any given nation. Just as longer life tends to correspond to better overall health in a population, it also aligns with overall quality of life. Therefore, the statistic is valuable in determining, in general, the level of a people's living standards.*

*In Antigua and Barbuda, the life expectancy in 2021 was estimated to be 77.55 years; 75.37 years for men, and 79.85 years for women. This figure ranked the country at number 84 in the world, out of 227. That means people in 83 nations could expect to live longer lives, on average, than Antiguans and Barbudans, but people in 143 nations fared worse. For comparison, that year, Japan was number 4 with a statistical life expectancy of 84.65; the United States was number 46, with a life expectancy of 80.43; and war-torn Afghanistan ranked 227th, with a life expectancy of 53.25 years.*

to education at all levels and have achieved a nearly universal literacy rate of 99.4 percent. Although girls are free to prepare for any careers they desire, cultural norms and expectations still play a role in determining their choices.

Women are more likely to be living in poverty than men (about 34 percent to 22 percent) and generally support larger households than men. The burden of poverty, therefore, falls more on women, who are more likely to work in seasonal, low-paid jobs. Correspondingly, their children grow up in poverty. Those children then go on to be more vulnerable to harmful outcomes in their teens, meaning they are more prone to become pregnant, drop out of school, and engage in dangerous behavior involving drugs and crime.

Organizations for women, such as the Professional Organization for Women of Antigua, have been formed to assist women in their careers. Throughout

the last couple of decades, more women are participating in government. Since 2004, when the first women were elected to the House of Representatives, women's involvement in political life had steadily increased. In the 2018 general elections, 2 women were elected to the House of Representatives; while in the Senate, 9 of the 18 members were women.

A scene of street life in Saint John's shows the warmth of a typical December day.

## VILLAGE LIFE

The majority of people in Antigua and Barbuda live in villages. Each village has a police station, a church (usually with an attached cemetery), a grocery store, retail stores, a primary school, a secondary school, and a medical clinic that is staffed every day of the week.

Students play steel drums at Holy Trinity Primary School and Nursery in Barbuda.

Farming and fishing are common in village life. Fishermen use nets, metal cages, and fishing poles to catch fish. They may also put on a snorkel mask, bend over the side of the boat, and take a look around in the water to spot conchs or lobsters. Crops such as fruits and vegetables are grown either to be sold to hotels or in Saint John's public market, or for personal consumption.

## EDUCATION

The country's educational system is based on the British system. It is a system with three tiers—primary, secondary, and tertiary. Education is free and compulsory from ages 5 to 16.

Each grade level is called a form. Prior to primary education, there are several preschools or preprimary schools for children ages 3 to 6. All preschools are privately owned. However, some government schools have begun to offer kindergarten classes.

Once primary education is completed, each student must take a national Primary School Examination to be able to pass on to secondary school. This test is taken at the age of 11 or 12, depending on the student's abilities.

In school, 10-year-old children learn such topics as social studies, which includes ecotourism; math, which includes addition, fractions, decimals, and percentages; and drug abuse resistance education.

Secondary school in Antigua and Barbuda lasts from four to five years. The age of secondary school students ranges from 11 or 12 to 18 years old. These students must complete five forms. Once the forms are complete, the students must take the examinations of the Caribbean Examination Council, which, upon completion, is equivalent to earning a North American high school diploma.

The University of the West Indies (UWI) is a public university system that serves the people of 17 English-speaking countries and territories in the Caribbean, including Antigua and Barbuda. With its main campus in Mona, Jamaica, UWI has five major university centers. Its newest, established in 2019, is UWI Five Islands, located on Antigua. This campus hosts the School of Humanities and Education; the School of Management, Science and Technology; and the School of Health and Behavourial Sciences, a nursing school.

In addition to UWI, there are several private, for-profit colleges operating in the country.

## PUBLIC TRANSPORTATION

There are two types of public transportation: buses and taxis. The majority of Antiguans take public buses, which begin their journey from the bus station next to the public market in Saint John's. Each bus is labeled with its destination. There is no timetable for bus departure and arrival. The bus driver simply leaves when the bus is full. This type of system makes it a challenge for people waiting at bus stops throughout the island. The buses usually run until 7:00 p.m.

Travelers wait at the West Bus Station Terminal in Antigua.

or 8:00 p.m., unless there is a big show in town. On Barbuda, there are no public buses.

Taxis are very expensive because all gas in the country is imported. Throughout Antigua, there are many gas stations, but on Barbuda, there is only one. The way to identify whether or not a van is a bus or a taxi is by its license plate. The license plate on a bus begins with the letters BUS and then a number, whereas a taxi's starts with the letters TX and then a number.

## MEDICAL CARE

Antigua and Barbuda has a well-developed health care system. To make it affordable, the Medical Benefits Scheme was established, which is paid for through payroll taxes. Chronic illnesses and diseases found to occur in the area are covered. These include diabetes, asthma, and heart disease.

Throughout the country, there are 26 health centers that provide general health care, as well as prenatal and postnatal care of mothers. The health of children is extremely important to the government of Antigua. Vaccinations against childhood diseases are mandatory. When a child begins school, the parents must provide records of the vaccinations that the child has gotten.

The main medical care facility in Antigua is the Mount St. John's Medical Center, a 185-bed teaching hospital that meets international standards for quality of health care. In addition, there are several private health-care facilities, including laboratories. There is a hospital on Barbuda, but it is very small, with only eight beds. If people need surgery or advanced procedures of any kind, they must be flown to Antigua. The hospital in Barbuda is mainly used for childbirth and for the dispensation of medication by a qualified doctor and pharmacist.

## INTERNET LINKS

**fiveislands.uwi.edu**
This is the site of the University of the West Indies Five Islands campus in Antigua.

**www.mbs.gov.ag/v2**
This is the homepage of Antigua's Medical Benefits Scheme.

**www.unicef.org/ECA_A_and_B_SitAn.pdf**
This publication takes an in-depth look at the status of children in Antigua and Barbuda.

# RELIGION

Saint John's Cathedral, an Anglican church also called
St. John the Divine, sits atop a hill in Saint John's, Antigua.
The cathedral dates to 1845 but is the site of two earlier
churches of the same name, the first one dating to 1681.

## 8

C HRISTIANITY IS THE MAIN RELIGION of Antigua and Barbuda. This dates to the times of British colonization. On Sunday, most Christian churches on the two islands are filled with people attending Sunday services. During the week, it is not uncommon for other services, such as Bible readings and seminars, to be offered.

More than three-quarters of the population is Christian. In the 2011 census, 68.3 percent of people identified as Protestant, with another 8.2 percent as Roman Catholic. The Anglican Church was historically dominant, but in 2011, it accounted for only 17.6 percent of the islands' faithful. Nevertheless, it remains the largest Protestant denomination, followed by Seventh-day Adventists, Pentecostals, Moravians, and Methodists. Before the abolition of slavery, the Anglican Church helped plantation owners, doing little to teach the enslaved people to read and write. In fact, they were often refused entry into churches.

## THE ANGLICAN COMMUNION

The name of the Anglican Church in Antigua and Barbuda is the Church in the Province of the West Indies. This church was established as self-governing in 1883 and consists of eight dioceses, or districts—two South American mainland dioceses and six island dioceses—all under the pastoral care of a bishop. Antigua and Barbuda belongs to the diocese

Antigua and Barbuda's constitution states that freedom of religion is a vital right of the country's citizens. This freedom is generally well respected, and there is little or no social discord based on religious differences.

**People pray during an Anglican service.**

of the North Eastern Caribbean and Aruba, which consists of 12 islands. The diocesan cathedral is Saint John's Cathedral in Saint John's, Antigua.

Those who worship in the Anglican Church consider themselves to be followers of Jesus Christ. The church asserts that its origins come from Jesus Christ and his apostles. Because the church is governed by bishops, it is also known as an Episcopal church.

The Anglican Communion is a worldwide association of all Anglican churches. Communion, in this usage, means a group of persons having a common religious faith. The Anglican Church is the third-largest Christian communion in the world, after the Roman Catholic Church and the Eastern Orthodox Church. It recognizes the Church of England as the original church. The religious head of the Church of England is the archbishop of Canterbury. Even though he has no power or authority outside of England, he is still considered the symbolic head of all Anglican churches.

Each church is run autonomously. However, any rites performed by one Anglican church are recognized by the others. Each church has the freedom to determine its own doctrine and religious ceremonies and its own legislative rules, overseen by a local bishop. The bishop responsible for the diocese of the North Eastern Caribbean and Aruba lives in Saint John's, Antigua. The membership for this diocese is about 60,000.

## MORAVIANS

The Moravians were the first to do missionary work among the enslaved people. During the 18th century, they worked hard to establish churches throughout the West Indies, such as in Saint Thomas, Saint Croix, and Antigua.

The Moravians' origins are based in ancient Bohemia and Moravia, which are now provinces of the Czech Republic. The church's precepts were begun by a rebel Catholic preacher named John Huss. He studied theology at the University of Prague and was appointed as a priest around 1400. While studying theology, Huss read the writings of John Wyclif, an English religious reformer. Even though Wyclif's writings were condemned by the University of Prague, Huss translated them into the Czech language.

As time passed, Huss developed many disagreements with the Roman Catholic Church and its practices. During his sermons, he attacked abuses of the Catholic Church before his congregation. He was excommunicated from the Catholic Church and forced into exile. At this time, he wrote many manuscripts that were influenced by Wyclif's writings.  He also refused to acknowledge the absolute power of the pope. He felt that the Bible should be the ruling law of any church. He was eventually accused of heresy by the Catholic Church and burned at the stake in 1415.

After his death, his followers established the Moravian Church in 1457. Up until 1722, most Moravians came from Bohemia and Moravia. After that time, the church's teachings began to spread throughout the world. The Moravian religion is considered to be one of the first Protestant religions.

A Moravian missionary, Samuel Isles, first arrived in Antigua in 1756. His purpose was to preach to the enslaved people. In Saint John's, the enslaved people would sit with a Moravian teacher under a sandbox tree on Sundays to begin their Sunday school lessons, which not only included Bible precepts, but also how to read and write. Moravian churches soon sprang up throughout the island, and by 1823, schools were attached to these churches.  By the time the enslaved people were freed, over half of them were converted Moravians.

## METHODISTS

Methodism has also been popular on the islands. One of its first missionaries was Nathanial Gilbert. He was born in Antigua in 1721 and was the son of an enslaver and plantation owner. When Gilbert got older, he went to England to study law before returning to Antigua.

Gilbert returned to England in 1758 after an illness. There, he was converted by John Wesley, an early leader in the Methodist movement. In 1759, Gilbert returned to Antigua and began preaching Methodism to enslaved people. Other missionaries soon followed. They taught about the spiritual equality of all people but urged enslaved people to obey their enslavers. Methodists also set up schools in various areas of the island. Today, the Moravian and Methodist churches are still well attended in Antigua.

## THE ANTIGUAN CHRISTIAN COUNCIL

In 1941, the Anglican, Methodist, Moravian, and Roman Catholic churches, along with the Salvation Army, joined together to form the Antigua Christian Council. The purpose of this council is to promote understanding and respect between different Christian groups.

Encouraging peace during politically unstable and troubled times is a very important aspect of this council. Prior to the 2004 election, the council created a code of ethics that promoted fair play and denounced any violence during

demonstrations or between groups. Each candidate in the election signed and agreed to the code of ethics.

In March 2020, the council temporarily suspended all services in member churches due to the COVID-19 pandemic.

## RASTAFARIANISM

Even though the Rastafarian hairstyle of dreadlocks is very common, there are only about 1,000 to 1,500 Antiguans and Barbudans who actively practice Rastafarianism. This religion gets its inspiration from a variety of sources. Followers read the Old Testament and the book of Revelation in the Bible. The majority of the Bible, though, is rejected by Rastafarians, who believe that its original context was altered. Instead, Rastafarians use the Holy Piby, also called the Black Man's Bible. In addition, they place special significance on an Ethiopian holy book called the Kebra Negast.

A man in Antigua wears the dreadlock hairstyle typical of Rastafarians.

The Ethiopian emperor Haile Selassie is considered a religious symbol for God incarnate by the Rastafarians. Selassie, however, was not a Rastafarian. Instead, he was a follower of the Ethiopian Orthodox Christian Church for his entire life.

The Rastafarian religion is also connected to Marcus Mosiah Garvey, a Jamaican who encouraged Black people to return to Africa, their rightful homeland. Garvey wanted the dignity of Black people restored to Africa. He told his followers that Africa would crown a great king and when that happened they would know that deliverance was upon them. The coronation of Selassie in 1930 is considered to be the fulfillment of Garvey's prophecy.

Rastafarians consider the use of cannabis (marijuana) to be a sacred part of their spiritual practice. Prior to 2018, when cannabis use was against the law in Antigua and Barbuda, Rastafarians were subject to arrest and occasionally harsh treatment at the hands of the police. They protested that the law discriminated against them and violated their religious freedom. In 2018, the country decriminalized cannabis, permitting adults to possess less than 15 grams, or four plants, for personal use only. At the time, Prime Minister Gaston Browne publicly apologized for the prior government treatment of Rastafarians.

## INTERNET LINKS

**www.anglicancommunion.org**
The Anglican Communion site explains its mission and theology, with relevant links to Antigua and Barbuda.

**www.moravian.org/mission/outreach/global-partners/eastern-west-indies**
The Moravian Church Eastern West Indies Province is presented on this page.

**www.state.gov/wp-content/uploads/2020/06/ANTIGUA-AND-BARBUDA-2019-INTERNATIONAL-RELIGIOUS-FREEDOM-REPORT.pdf**
This pdf is the 2019 U.S. State Department report on religious freedom in Antigua and Barbuda.

# LANGUAGE

ANTIGUA & BARBUDA
NATIONAL PARK

## Thank You For Visiting!

A sign in English welcomes visitors to
Nelson's Dockyard in English Harbour.

ENGLISH IS THE OFFICIAL LANGUAGE of Antigua and Barbuda. However, most people are bilingual and grow up speaking Antiguan Creole. This mix of English and West African languages is also called Leeward Caribbean Creole English. Variations of this language are spoken in the Leeward Island countries of Antigua and Barbuda, Saint Kitts and Nevis, and the British territories of Anguilla and Montserrat. Antiguan Creole developed during British rule as a way for plantation owners and enslaved Africans to communicate with each other—hence, it is a hybrid, or mix, of their languages.

Standard English is the language used in schools and by the government, and Antiguan Creole is used in everyday speech. Most people on the islands can switch from English to Creole quite easily.

## ANTIGUAN CREOLE

Linguists, or specialists in the science of languages, who have studied Antiguan Creole have found very definite West African words in the

A *creole* is a language that developed over time from mixing two or more languages into a new one. It's often spoken by a community whose ancestors were displaced geographically so that their ties to their original language and culture were partly broken, often the result of slavery. Creoles are characterized by a consistent system of grammar and a large stable vocabulary, and they are learned by children as their mother tongue.

language. In addition, many English words are pronounced somewhat differently. For example, the word "give" becomes *gee* in Antiguan Creole. Such Creole words came about because some African languages do not have a sound for "v" or "th." This made it difficult for enslaved Africans to pronounce words with these sounds. Words were changed to omit these sounds: "think" is pronounced as *tink*; "live" is *lib*.

The Antiguan pronunciation is quite similar to what is spoken in Jamaica. This could be because the enslaved people of these countries came from the same place in Africa. Here are some examples of pronunciation patterns:

- TR as in "truck" is pronounced CH, thus: *chruck*.
- DR as in "dress" is pronounced J, thus: *jess*.
- TH in "them" is pronounced D, thus: *dem*.
- TH in "think" is pronounced T, thus: *tink*.

A steel-drum player greets cruise ship passengers arriving in Saint John's.

- WN as in "down" is pronounced NG, thus: *dung*.
- V as in "vex" is pronounced B, thus: *bex*.
- Sometimes a final T sound is left off, and words such as "best" are spoken as *bess*; "expect" sounds like *expeck*; and "left" sounds like *leff*.

English grammar usages are also altered in Antiguan Creole. For example, "He is my father" might become "Him my father," which omits the verb "is" and uses an objective pronoun as the subject. Possessive pronouns are sometimes replaced by an objective pronoun, for instance, "You walk to my house" might be changed to "You walk me house." Not only is the pronoun changed, but the preposition "to" is also left out.

There are also many West African expressions in Antiguan Creole. *Bassabassa* means "fooling around." *Catta* is a cloth that is placed on the head to help in carrying a large or heavy load. A man who is easily manipulated

| Antiguan Creole | Standard English |
| --- | --- |
| "Me na know weydatdey!" | "I don't know where it is!" |
| "Smady" | "Somebody" |
| "Breeze off" | "Take a rest" |
| "Down wet-up" | "Throw water at" |
| "Wagy" | "Clothes" |
| "Wey you a go?" | "Where are you going?" |
| "Na badda me" | "Don't bother me" |
| "She garn a choch" | "She has gone to church" |
| "Wey de food garn?" | "Where has the food gone?" |
| "Me na min no" | "I do not know" |
| "Sen de money giee me" | "Send me the money" |
| "Me nartek um" | "I am not taking it" |
| "Whey it drop it tap" | "I will use up what I have now" |

by a woman is called a *kunumunu*. These are just a few of the West African expressions that have found their way into the language.

## MASS MEDIA

The government-owned Antigua and Barbuda Broadcasting Service (ABS) provides radio and television to the two islands. Some other broadcasting services are Observer Radio, Radio ZDK, the Baptist-run Caribbean Radio Lighthouse, and the BBC World Service. The majority of households in the country own a TV and radio.

*The Daily Observer*, which was the island nation's only daily newspaper in recent years, went to online-only publication in 2018.

The internet is widely available and used. In 2018, around 76 percent of the population used the internet.

## INTERNET LINKS

**blog.virginatlantic.com/a-caribbean-dictionary**
This article celebrates various Caribbean dialects, including that of Antigua and Barbuda.

**www.britannica.com/topic/creole-languages**
*Britannica* covers the topic of Creole languages in general.

**www.dandc.eu/en/article/creole-languages-caribbean-reflect-and-express-peoples-identities**
This article discusses the linguistic heritage of the Caribbean islands.

ARTS

A woman walks past a display of paintings for sale in Saint John's.

## 10

THE CARIBBEAN SUNLIGHT, WATER, and landscape evoke a colorful artistic sensibility in Antigua. The region's distinctive cultural mix of West African and European influences is expressed in a variety of arts and crafts.

A pottery shop in Redcliffe Quay displays its wares.

The original people of both Antigua and Barbuda left behind artifacts dating back around 5,000 years. These relics include stone, bone, and shell tools. Later people dating to about 500 BCE, called the Saladoid, produced sophisticated pottery.

Many artists live and work in Antigua. Some maintain studios and sell their works to tourists and local art galleries; others set up handicraft stalls at outdoor markets. Paintings and other visual artworks are often characterized by bright colors and island themes.

The islanders' love of bright colors and exuberant expression is especially displayed at festival times. Carnival is the biggest celebration of the year, with brilliant costumes, dance, and music. Music, in particular, is Antigua's most popular form of expression and creativity.

## MUSIC

Music is very important to Antiguans and Barbudans and can be heard everywhere. A wide variety of music exists, including reggae, jazz, hip-hop, gospel, steel pan, and calypso, with West Indian rhythms being predominant.

A man plays a drum while busking for donations on a street in Saint John's.

**CALYPSO** Perhaps the most popular music is calypso. Although this genre is most often associated with Trinidad and Tobago, it's also popular throughout the eastern Caribbean and is an important part of the culture in Antigua and Barbuda. Its distinctive syncopated 2/4 or 4/4 rhythms—which harken back to West African *kaiso* music—are easy to dance to and very entertaining. Despite the upbeat sound, however, calypso lyrics can be quite scathing, addressing controversial subjects of the day. Calypso artists, or *calypsonians*, freely comment on local political situations or social problems. Calypso performers are not only singers but also actors who use dramatic gestures to entertain.

# CHARACTERISTICS OF CALYPSO MUSIC

*Like many forms of Caribbean music, calypso merges the rhythmic traditions of West Africa with the musical influences of Spain, France, England, and other European nations. Typically, the main elements of calypso include:*

- *Folk origins: Many calypso songs are interpretations of old folk songs.*

- *Creole lyrics: Calypso performers sing in the everyday language of their homeland.*

- *A griot: The lead singer, once called a chantwell, uses a call-and-response format to engage the audience. In African traditions, this storyteller-poet was the griot, or oral historian. The lead singer is now referred to as the calypsonian.*

- *Steel drums: Calypso bands include a variety of instruments, including guitars, trumpets, and Latin percussion, but the most iconic are steel pan drums.*

The roots of calypso reach back to the times of slavery. Africans were often not allowed to talk to each other while working on the plantations. To communicate or talk about the hard times they had to endure, the people sang. These songs were not necessarily composed by a single person; rather, they evolved with lyrics about current social or economic situations.

The music became popular throughout the Caribbean in the 19th and 20th centuries. It spawned many related musical genres, including benna—which is most associated with Antigua and Barbuda—soca, reggae, and other Caribbean music styles.

Probably the best known Antiguan calypso singer is MacLean Emanuel, better known as King Short Shirt. He rose to fame in the 1960s and won many competitions in Antigua, where he was considered a Calypso Monarch, or king. His 1976 hit "Tourist Leggo" placed second at the Trinidad and Tobago Carnival Road March, the Caribbean's most prestigious calypso competition.

Claudette Peters is a popular Antiguan soca and soul singer-songwriter, known for hits such as "Something Got a Hold on Me." The name "soca" derives from SOul of CAlypso, and it tends to incorporate more electronic instrumentation. A former winner of the Miss Teenager Pageant at Antigua's

*Located in Saint John's old courthouse, the Museum of Antigua and Barbuda is devoted to safeguarding the islands' history. It was opened in 1985 and is run by the Historical and Archaeological Society. Its exhibits tell the story of Antigua and Barbuda's natural, social, and political history. Throughout the years, it has collected many historical objects and has compiled a vast database of information.*

*The museum also has an educational program. Lectures are given to schoolchildren about history, and it also organizes field trips to visit historical sites. In addition, it organizes cultural evenings for the general public.*

Carnival, Peters came to be known as the island nation's Soca Diva. In January 2021, she performed at a special event to honor the inauguration of Kamala Harris as the first Black vice president of the United States. Harris's father is Jamaican, and the Caribbean people therefore celebrate Kamala Harris as one of their own. The concert was broadcast across the Caribbean by One Caribbean Television.

**BENNA** This traditional folk song genre in Antigua and Barbuda emerged as a type of popular music during the era of slavery. Songs are based on gossip and rumor and are delivered in a call-and-response format. Lyrical themes are typically of praise, ridicule, or women. The singers make up the words to the songs as they go along and are often accompanied by drums. Years ago,

Steel drums are on display at V. C. Bird International Airport in Antigua.

these types of songs brought mental and emotional relief to the enslaved Africans working in the fields and gave them a means to express their ideas and opinions. Benna music was therefore a useful form of spreading news and information across the island.

One of the most famous benna singers lived in the middle of the 20th century. His name was John Quarkoo. He was known for making public announcements, relaying the latest gossip, or singing about up-to-date topics, always with satire and wit. He ridiculed the oppressors of the Black Antiguans and even found himself in jail with the charge of slander. This talented benna singer made up his lyrics on the spot.

During the 1940s and 1950s, benna was the main nonreligious music in Antigua and Barbuda. It was later replaced by Trinidad Calypso, which has strong rhythms with energetic ballads that deal with current affairs through satire. Because of the historical importance of benna, it is still played today at cultural events.

## ANTIGUAN WRITERS

The theme of most Antiguan writers is island life. Jamaica Kincaid is probably the most famous author who was born in Antigua. She has written novels, short stories, and essays about her life in Antigua. Some of her novels are *Annie John* (1984), *Lucy* (1990), and *The Autobiography of My Mother* (1996). Her memoir *A Small Place* (1988) takes a harsh look at the effects of colonialism on her homeland. *My Brother* (1997) is an account of her brother's death from AIDS.

She was born in 1949 as Elaine Potter Richardson. She lived with her mother and stepfather until she left Antigua in 1965 to live in New York. She completed her secondary education there and continued her education at Franconia College in New Hampshire. She changed her name to Jamaica Kincaid in 1973. She worked as a staff writer for *The New Yorker* magazine for many years, where her essays often focused on Caribbean culture. Today, she is the Professor of African and African American Studies in Residence at Harvard University during the academic year and spends her summers in North Bennington, Vermont.

Joanne C. Hillhouse is another contemporary Antiguan author. Her books include books for children, young adults, and adults. They include

*The Boy from Willow Bend* (2002), *Dancing Nude in the Moonlight* (2004), and *Musical Youth* (2014). She also helped produce Antigua and Barbuda's first and second feature films, *The Sweetest Mango* and *No Seed*. Hillhouse has been involved in television production and freelance journalism for local publications. In 2004, Hillhouse founded Wadadli Pen, a fiction writing contest for young people in Antigua and Barbuda. The organization sponsors literary contests, workshops, and arts showcases to encourage and sustain arts opportunities for youth.

## INTERNET LINKS

**antiguahistory.net/Museum/prehistoric.htm**
Examples of ancient indigenous artifacts can be seen on this site.

**www.antiguamuseums.net**
This is the home site of the Museum of Antigua and Barbuda.

**www.blackpast.org/african-american-history/kincaid-jamaica-1949**
This site presents a quick biography of Jamaica Kincaid.

**calypsoglobal.weebly.com/king-short-shirt---antiguas-living-legend.html**
A biography of King Short Shirt is presented on this calypso site.

**wadadlipen.wordpress.com**
The Wadadli Pen website showcases its activities.

# LEISURE

**Sailboats race in the blue waters of the Caribbean Sea during a regatta in Antigua.**

**11**

BEING AN ISLAND NATION, ANTIGUA and Barbuda naturally lends itself to water activities. Tourists come for the beaches, the regattas, and the fishing. They enjoy sailing, scuba diving, snorkeling, jet skiing, and waterskiing, as well as the land-based pleasures of golf, tennis, and basking in luxurious spas. The people who live on the islands also enjoy these pastimes if they have the money and the leisure time.

However, the working people live more ordinary lives, often aimed at catering to the leisure needs of tourists and wealthy residents. Like most people, they use their leisure time to get together with family and friends, play some games, watch sports, or fire up some good food, music, and dancing.

## SPORTS

In Antigua and Barbuda, there are professional sports played in beautiful stadiums and pick-up games of football (soccer) played in fields shared with grazing goats. Soccer and basketball are favorite sports, but without question, the most beloved sport is the British game of cricket, which is popular throughout the Caribbean.

**CRICKET**   Cricket originally came to the West Indies during colonial times. British military officials established cricket clubs (for white people only) in the early 19th century, but over time, the game was embraced by the Black population, though the teams remained segregated at first.

Today, cricket fans in Antigua and Barbuda are fiercely devoted and often pack the stadiums during cricket matches. International matches are televised so everyone can watch the games. Cricket season begins in Antigua during the month of January and lasts through July. The national stadium in Saint John's is called the Antigua Recreation Ground, also known as the Old Recreation Ground or Old Rec. In addition, the newer Sir Vivian Richards Stadium, named for the nation's greatest cricket player, opened in North Sound, Antigua, in 2006. Problems with the field there, however, as well as the stadium's out-of-the-way location, have prevented the newer stadium from gaining popularity with the fans.

Women enjoy playing cricket as well, and the Antigua and Barbuda Softball Cricket Association oversees teams for women and girls. Local teams compete against each other and then go on to play against women's teams from throughout the Caribbean islands.

**HOW CRICKET IS PLAYED**   This game started centuries ago as a simple game of batting an object, such as a piece of wood, between two players. It evolved into a game with 11 players on each team. A cricket ball and bat are used during the game. A cricket ball is a little bit smaller but heavier than a baseball. The cricket bat is wooden and measures 38 inches (96.5 cm) long by 4.25 inches (10.8 cm) wide. The bat has a handle and a flat wooden paddle called a blade.

Cricket can be played on a grassy field or in a stadium. The central rectangular area is called a pitch and is 22 yards (20 m) long. Two standing wickets are placed at either end of the pitch. The wickets consist of three vertical sticks that are 2.5 feet (75 cm) high and called stumps, with two small horizontal pieces called bails resting on top of them.

Each team has a chance to bat. When one team is up to bat, the other team is in the field, except for a bowler, whose role is similar to the pitcher in

## SIR VIVIAN RICHARDS

*Known as the "Master Blaster" of world-class cricket, Vivian Richards began playing cricket professionally in 1974. In 1975, he helped his West Indies team win its first international title at the Cricket World Cup in England. The teams playing were England, Australia, New Zealand, the West Indies, India, Pakistan, Sri Lanka, and East Africa. The final match was between Australia and the West Indies, and the Windies won by 17 runs. The team won the next Cricket World Cup in 1979 as well, and Richards was named Man of the Match.*

*Richards went on to serve as captain of the West Indies team from 1984 to 1991. Over the course of his career, he set many international records. Now retired, Richards is still revered in Antigua today. The Museum of Antigua and Barbuda is home to his cricket bat. Because of his outstanding record, he received an honorary knighthood, and he is now referred to as Sir Vivian Richards. He is considered one of the top five cricket players in the world.*

A statue of Sir Vivian Richards depicts him victoriously holding up a cricket bat.

baseball. Two batsmen are up at one time. They are positioned on opposite ends of the pitch. One of the batsmen is up to bat, or "on strike," while another waits to make a run. The bowler pitches the ball at the batting batsman. The bowler tries to aim the ball at the bails to knock them off or to strike the batter out. If the batsman hits the ball hard enough, he and the waiting batsmen can make a run. The batting team scores when both batsmen run to their opposite wickets. The winning team is the one with the highest number of runs.

## SAILING

Because Antigua and Barbuda are surrounded by water and have continuous trade winds, sailing is very popular. In the past, sailing was the only means of

**A J-Class racing yacht passes a competitor in the Antigua Classic Yacht Regatta.**

traveling long distances across the sea. Today, sailing is a sport, and boating enthusiasts come from all over the world to take part in the regattas in Antigua and Barbuda. There are two yacht clubs in Antigua—the Antigua Yacht Club and the Jolly Harbour Yacht Club.

**ANTIGUA SAILING WEEK** The end of April and beginning of May is Antigua Sailing Week, which takes place over five days. (In 2021, it was canceled because of the COVID-19 pandemic.) Typically, around 5,000 people come to watch about 1,500 people race 200 sailboats—some of the biggest and fastest sailing yachts in the world. It is known as the largest regatta in the Caribbean, as well as one of the top three regattas in the world.

Billowing white sails blow in the wind as the sail boats creak and sway in the blue waters of the Caribbean. Races such as Dickenson Bay Race, Jolly Harbour Race, Ocean Race, and Bareboat Challenge are held. Trophies are awarded to the winners of these races. Top-class judges with experience at Olympic regattas and world championships monitor the events. One of these is the Antigua Classic Yacht Regatta, dedicated to older style vessels.

## GAMES

**WARRI** Antigua and Barbuda's national board game is *warri*, meaning "house." Warri is a thinking game like chess and backgammon, but it most resembles mancala. It was brought to the West Indies by enslaved people from West Africa during the sugar era.

The warri game board is a rectangular wooden board that is sometimes very ornately carved. It has 12 hollows, or houses, designed with 6 on each side. At each end of the board are larger houses for capturing the nickars, which are small nuts found in the Antiguan bush.

It is played by two opponents. They both start with 24 counters, or nickars. The players place 4 nickars in each of their 6 houses on the board, making the total nickars on the board 48. To win, one player must capture 25 nickars. This is accomplished by a variety of techniques, such as a quick ability to calculate, verbal pressure, and skillful movements.

Fish designs adorn this wooden warri game board in Saint John's.

Warri has become part of the Mind Sports Olympiad, which is a festival featuring more than 40 different thinking games. The Mind Sports Olympiad organization is based in London, England. In Antigua, the National Warri Festival is held in October. During the festival, the best players are determined and an overall champion is named. Warri is also played throughout the year at various rum shops in Antigua.

**DOMINOES** Another popular pastime game is dominoes. This game is played in nearly all the villages around Antigua and Barbuda and is an international game. Recently, Trevor Simon won the Antiguan championship and represented Antigua in a major domino tournament held in England. There are many variations to this game, but the most common version uses 28 domino pieces. The domino pieces are placed facedown on the table and then shuffled around by the players. There are usually two players, and each selects seven dominoes.

One player starts by placing a domino on the table face up. The opponent must lay a domino with the same value next to the first domino with the like value sides touching. Then, the other player must do the same, and so on. The winner is the first person to run out of dominoes.

## INTERNET LINKS

**antiguaclassics.com**
**www.sailingweek.com**
These sites provide information and photos relating to yacht racing in Antigua.

**blog.virginatlantic.com/sir-vivian-richards-king-of-antigua-cricket**
This article spotlights Antigua's greatest cricket star, Sir Vivian Richards.

**healthy.uwaterloo.ca/museum/VirtualExhibits/countcap/pages/warri.html**
This site explains the game of warri.

**www.telegraph.co.uk/travel/destinations/caribbean/antigua-and-barbuda/articles/on-the-trail-of-cricketing-history-in-antigua**
This travel article is written from the perspective of a visiting cricket fan in Antigua.

# FESTIVALS

Two women cook cassava pancakes on an open-air grill during an Independence Day celebration in Saint John's.

**12**

R ELIGIOUS FESTIVALS, PATRIOTIC and historical anniversaries, and cultural traditions mark the important celebrations in Antigua and Barbuda. The major Christian festivals of Good Friday, Easter Monday, Whit Monday, and Christmas are important holidays, and the remaining public holidays are secular. These are New Year's Day (January 1), Labour Day (early May), Independence Day (November 1), and V. C. Bird Day (December 9). Carnival marks the emancipation of enslaved people on August 1, 1834, and is a huge, multiday celebration.

In addition to public holidays, there are many local and national festivals that take place during the year, such as the Antigua International Hot Air Balloon Festival, Antigua Sun Annual Kite Flying Competition, Antigua Sailing Week, Heritage Day, and Wadadli Day, a festival that was added in 1997 to market the islands' homegrown and homemade products. Wadadli Day was created to celebrate everything Antiguan, including national costumes. It is held in the Botanical Gardens in Saint John's. All

food, dress, and entertainment at this celebration is indigenous to Antigua.

## CARNIVAL

This festival celebrates emancipation and lasts for about 10 days. All Antiguans, young and old, celebrate from July through to the beginning of August. Celebrators wear costumes made from a rainbow of colors, such as pink, purple, green, red, turquoise, orange, blue, silver, and gold. During the festival, talent shows are held, as well as a parade of bands. There are several beauty pageants, and the biggest honor of all is to be crowned the Carnival Queen. Once crowned, the Carnival Queen reigns for one year. During this time, she is a traveling ambassador for Antigua.

Calypso music is an important part of Carnival. During the festivals, calypso competitions are some of the main events. The last competition in Carnival determines who will wear the Calypso Monarch's crown. The winner is crowned late on Sunday night or sometimes very early Monday morning.

Ornate costumes such as this woman's add to the festive atmosphere of Carnival.

The French word *J'ouvert* describes the biggest event of the Carnival celebration. The word translates as "I open," but roughly means, "This is your last chance to celebrate, so live it up!" The J'ouvert begins on the first Monday in August at 4:00 a.m., when Antiguans swarm into the streets. Everybody begins to dance along the streets of Saint John's. Decorative floats and bands

## THE HISTORY OF CHRISTMAS IN ANTIGUA

*Antiguans have always loved the Christmas season. In the past, the Christmas season began about three weeks before Christmas Day. It started with carol singers carrying a carol tree throughout Saint John's. A carol tree was constructed of wood with crossbars that acted as arms for hanging lanterns.*

*The week before Christmas saw the most activity, with masqueraders walking the streets and music being played everywhere. Acrobats and tumblers performed dressed in colorful and sometimes silly costumes. At home, women made a new dress for each of the three days of Christmas. This was a time when everyone was dressed in their Sunday best.*

*Other past Christmas traditions were long ghosts and John Bulls. Long ghosts were scary-looking, 12-foot-high (3.6 m) masked figures on stilts. These masqueraders roamed the streets to get donations for Christmas.*

*The character John Bull originated as a political cartoon. He supposedly represented England (or British plantation owners) in a satirical way. Men who dressed up as John Bull in Antigua and Barbuda wore ugly masks similar to those of African witch doctors. Their heads were topped with bull horns. The intent was to look as grotesque as possible. John Bulls would terrorize and excite anyone around them. A cattle tender or another person next to a John Bull carried a whip. He would crack it over the John Bull's head, making the John Bull run toward the screaming audience. Even though John Bulls no longer come out during the Christmas season, they can sometimes still be seen during Carnival festivities or during a jump up in the villages when there is a long weekend holiday.*

make their way through the crowds. The final street dancing lasts from dusk to midnight on the first Tuesday in August, when Carnival is officially over.

## V. C. BIRD/NATIONAL HEROES DAY

December 9 is V. C. Bird Day, and the date marks his birthday in 1910. Vere Cornwall Bird was the first prime minister of Antigua and Barbuda and is considered the "Father of the Nation." In 2004, when the country was under the political rule of Bird's opposition party, the holiday was renamed National

A ribbon-bedecked Christmas tree decorates a shopping area in Heritage Quay in Saint John's during the holiday season.

Heroes Day and expanded to honor five other important figures in the country's history. Various National Heroes Days are celebrated across the Caribbean.

However, in 2014, with yet another political flip in leadership, the holiday was reinstated as V. C. Bird Day. A day to honor the other national heroes was created on October 26, but it was not, at that point, a public holiday. Whether the status of this commemoration will change again with another turn of the political tide remains to be seen.

The other national heroes of Antigua and Barbuda (as of 2021) include King Court Tackey (Prince Klaas), the leader of an 18th-century revolt by enslaved people; Nellie Robinson, a pioneer in education; Viv Richards, a celebrated cricket player; George Herbert Walter, a former prime minister; and Lester Bird, the country's second prime minister and the son of Vere Bird.

## CHRISTMAS TODAY

Christmas season in Antigua begins in late November when all the radio stations begin to play Christmas songs. Christmas bazaars selling arts and crafts are set up at schools and churches. The streets of Saint John's are adorned with Christmas decorations. Homes are also decorated with Christmas trees and lights. Christmas programs, pageants, and carol services are held at schools and churches, reciting, acting, and singing about the story of Christmas.

Souse, or headcheese, is often eaten on Christmas Eve. This cheese is more like a jellied loaf. It is called headcheese because it is made from the meaty parts from the head of a pig. The pig's trotters (feet) are also included. The headcheese is prepared by simmering the head until the meat falls off and the liquid becomes a jellylike broth. The meat is chopped, seasoned, and then put back in the broth, which is then placed in a mold and chilled until it is firm.

A local drink prepared only during Christmas is called sorrel. It comes from the herb of that name, which grows flowers with red petals. These petals are removed and put into a glass jar with cinnamon, hot water, and a few grains of rice. This mixture could be left fermenting for days or weeks.

Sometimes, on Christmas Eve (December 24), a fundraising drive is organized. The drive is fun and lively, more like a party with food for sale and local entertainment.

Breakfast on Christmas is usually ham, eggs, and bread. Making the Christmas dinner is an important part of the day. Food such as roasted turkey, ham, or a beef roast; candied sweet potatoes; peas and rice; salad; and Christmas cake and pudding might be prepared for the Christmas feast.

On Old Year's Night, which is December 31, a Bush Tea party is planned that starts at around 8 p.m. A variety of teas are served. Some are made from local plants found in the bush. Foods such as ham rolls, sausage, and cheese are also provided.

## INTERNET LINKS

**www.caribbeanandco.com/things-to-know-about-antigua-carnival**
Many photos accompany this detailed article about Carnival in Antigua.

**www.caribbean-beat.com/issue-22/caribbean-christmas#axzz6mqZYUqD6**
This article takes a look at Christmas traditions in Antigua and elsewhere in the Caribbean.

**www.timeanddate.com/holidays/antigua-and-barbuda**
This calendar site provides up-to-date annual listings of public holidays in Antigua and Barbuda.

**A wide array of produce is displayed for sale at the Saint John's farmers' market.**

13

THE FOODS OF THE CARIBBEAN ARE similar throughout the islands. The cuisine is a mix of African, Amerindian, and European traditions, with Latin American, Indian/South Asian, Middle Eastern, and Chinese influences. The food reflects the geographical location of the islands—featuring tropical fruits and vegetables—as well as the historical and economic forces that have impacted Caribbean life over the years. In recent years, international chain restaurants and fast food items aimed at tourists have popped up across the region.

However, while certain foods and flavors are common throughout the Caribbean—including conch, plantain, coconut, saltfish, sweet potato, rice and beans, and goat—individual islands have their own specialties.

## ICONIC DISHES

Antigua's quintessential dishes are the standard fare of home cooking but are also found at roadside stands and on restaurant menus.

The famous Antiguan black pineapple is not actually black. It is much like a regular pineapple but smaller, and its flesh is more golden. It's said to be the world's sweetest pineapple, and its core is edible. The fruit is grown mainly on the south side of Antigua and is sold only locally. Roadside vendors sell these special treats to tourists and local people alike.

Pepperpot is a stew of meat scraps, local vegetables, and spicy peppers. Although the dish is popular throughout the Caribbean, it's often heralded as Antigua's national dish.

Fungee, sometimes spelled *fungi* or *fungie*, is a cornmeal mush often made with okra. It's often called Antiguan polenta since it resembles the Italian cornmeal mush. Fungee is served on its own, often for breakfast, and is mandatory with pepperpot. Either way, it's also considered a national dish.

Ducana is a particularly Antiguan dish. It's a mash of grated, spiced sweet potato and coconut, cooked tamale-style, wrapped in banana leaves and steamed in simmering water. Ducana is often served with saltfish.

Conch is the meat of the mollusk that lives in the spiraled conch shell. Batter-dipped and deep-fried is just one way it is enjoyed on the island.

Goat water is a curried stew or soup made with goat meat.

*Fungee and pepperpot is considered the national dish of Antigua and Barbuda. Pepperpot, which is popular throughout the Caribbean, is a stew made of beef and/or pork, yam, pumpkin, peas, okra, eggplant, plantain, dasheen leaves (similar to spinach), and squash. In Antigua and Barbuda, this is served with fungee (also spelled fungi or fungie), a kind of mush made of cornmeal and okra.*

*This national dish is thought to have originated from the Amerindians living long ago in Antigua. They would have made the stew in a deep clay firepot that was used for food storage. Later, the enslaved African on the islands made this dish with inexpensive meat scraps—such as cows' feet and pigs' tails and snouts—with local vegetables and hot spices. They served it with the fungee, to provide a filling and nourishing dish of protein and carbohydrates.*

Fungee and pepperpot is a favorite dish in **Antigua** and **Barbuda**.

**Tasty jerk chicken, salad, and rice with beans is another favorite dish in Antigua.**

Souse is a cold, refreshing soup of pickled pigs' feet, hot peppers, and lime. It's particularly popular during the festival of Carnival.

Macaroni pie is beloved throughout the West Indies. It's a type of mac and cheese that is served in slices or squares, and it is sometimes served cold. It is typically made with grated cheddar cheese, evaporated milk, and egg and is standard fare at lunchtime, picnics, and Sunday dinners.

These dishes are enjoyed with soft buttery bread and salads of tropical fruits and vegetables.

## BEVERAGES

Thirsty Antiguans enjoy a variety of fresh fruit juices, including mango, raspberry, passion fruit, guava, tamarind, soursop, and lemonade. Seamoss is a popular drink, a frothy, creamy beverage made from agar, a type of seaweed.

## RUM

*Because of Antigua and Barbuda's sugar plantation history, rum has been made there since the mid-1700s. Rum was very important during the colonial era, especially for medical purposes. Even though Nelson's Dockyard had a medical facility, the main medicine used there was rum.*

*This alcoholic beverage is made by distilling fermented sugar and water. The sugar, of course, comes from sugarcane and is fermented from either molasses or cane juice.*

*Molasses is made when brown sugar is produced. Once the sugarcane juice has been boiled and all the crystallized sugar has been removed, a sweet, sticky by-product remains.*

*Fermented sugar is created by taking cane juice or molasses and mixing it with water. This mixture is then fermented and distilled, which produces alcohol. The alcohol is then placed in oak barrels and aged from 2 to 30 years or more.*

*In the early days, rum in Antigua consisted of different homemade brews. Then, mass-produced Cavalier rums began to be made in the 1950s. The first one was called Cavalier Muscovado Rum. Today, a variety of Cavalier rums can still be found throughout the island.*

Mauby is a somewhat bitter but refreshing drink made from the bark and leaves of the mauby tree. Ginger beer, hibiscus tea, and coconut milk are also typical everyday drinks.

## INTERNET LINKS

**eatyourworld.com/destinations/central_america_and_caribbean/antigua_and_barbuda**
This travel site offers photos and descriptions of local Antiguan specialties.

**www.sandals.com/blog/antigua-food-drinks-3**
A resort offers a list of popular Antiguan foods with photos.

# SALTFISH (SALT COD WITH PEPPERS AND ONIONS)

1 pound (454 grams) salted cod fish
¼ cup (60 milliliters) cooking oil
1 medium onion, peeled, sliced into rings
1 bell pepper (green, red, or yellow), sliced
2 cloves garlic, chopped
1 tablespoon fresh thyme leaves (or
  1 teaspoon dried thyme)
1 8-ounce can (225 g) tomato sauce
2 tablespoons apple cider vinegar
1 tablespoon butter
black pepper, to taste

Soak the fish in water for about 4 hours or overnight.

Boil fish in fresh water for 45 minutes.

Place fish in cold water until cool enough to handle. Break fish into bite-size pieces, removing as many bones as possible.  Set aside.

Pour oil in frying pan, and add the onion and peppers. Sauté until soft. Add garlic, and stir a minute longer.

Add tomato sauce, fish, vinegar, and butter, and cook over low heat, stirring occasionally. Add black pepper to taste.

Serve with ducana or fungee and chopped vegetables, such as spinach and eggplant.

# DUCANA (SPICED SWEET POTATO COCONUT DUMPLING)

1 cup (120 g) finely grated raw, peeled
 sweet potato
¾ cup (85 g) fresh grated coconut
½ cup (60 g) granulated sugar
2 tablespoons unsalted butter, room temperature
1 teaspoon cinnamon
1 teaspoon vanilla
¾ teaspoon nutmeg
¼ teaspoon salt
¼ cup (30 g) raisins (optional)
1—1 ½ cups (120—180 g) all purpose flour
¼ cup (60 mL) water
Banana leaves or aluminum foil

Bring a large pot of unsalted water to a boil.

In a large bowl, combine the grated sweet potato and coconut. Mix in the sugar, butter, cinnamon, vanilla, nutmeg, and raisins.

Mix in just enough flour to form a soft dough. If it is too dry, gradually add a small amount of water (up to a ¼ cup).

If using banana leaves, cut them into 6-inch (15 cm) squares. Rinse the banana leaves under hot water until they are pliable. Alternatively, cut foil squares.

Place about ½ cup of dough into the center of a banana leaf square and form into a rectangle or cylinder. Fold the leaf over the dough to cover on all sides, then wrap with kitchen twine to secure. Repeat with remaining dough. If using foil, do the same, but there's no need for twine. Just be sure to fold the packets very securely.

Lower the heat to bring the water to a gentle boil. Add the packets of dough, and simmer for about 45 minutes. Remove from the pot, and allow the packets to cool for 10 minutes before unwrapping. Serve warm or at room temperature.

# A

# B

# C

# D

## 1

*Goat Island*

*Hog Point*

*Two Feet Bay*

**ATLANTIC OCEAN**

*Codrington Lagoon*

*Rubbish Bay*

*Low Bay*

● Codrington

*The Highlands*

**Barbuda**

*Palmetto Point*

*Pelican Bay*

*Salt Pond*

## 2

## Caribbean Sea

## 3

International boundary
Regional boundary
● Capital city
● Major town
▲ Mountain peak

| Feet | | Meters |
|---|---|---|
| 1,650 | | 500 |
| 660 | | 200 |
| 0 | | 0 |

**N**

## 4

*Dickenson Bay*

**PARISH OF ST. JOHN**

**PARISH OF ST. GEORGE**

*Jumby Bay*

*Great Bird Island*

*Pillar Book Bay*

*North Sound*

*Galley Bay*

*Guiana Island*

*Hawksbill Bay*

ST. JOHN'S

**PARISH OF ST. PETER**

*Crump Island*

*Devil's Bridge*

*Five Islands Harbour*

**Antigua**

● Willikies

*Ayres Creek*

*Lignumvitae Bay*

**PARISH OF ST. MARY**

Potworks Dam

**PARISH OF ST. PHILIP**

*Green Island*

Boggy Peak (1,319 ft /402 m)

▲

**PARISH OF ST. PAUL**

*Willoughby Bay*

*Half Moon Bay*

*Wallings Forest*

*Cades Bay*

*Carlisle Bay*

*Falmouth Harbour*

## 5

◗ Redonda

Atlantic Ocean, D1

Boggy Peak, C5

Cades Bay, C5
Carlisle Bay, C5
Codrington, C1
Codrington Lagoon, C1
Crump Island, D4

Devil's Bridge, D4
Dickenson Bay, C4

Falmouth Harbour, D5
Five Islands Harbour, C4

Galley Bay, C4

Goat Island, C1
Great Bird Island, D4
Green Island, D4, D5
Guiana Island, D4

Half Moon Bay, D5
Hawksbill Bay, C4
The Highlands, D1
Hog Point, D1

Jumby Bay, D4

Lignumvitae Bay, C4, C5
Low Bay, C1

Palmetto Point, C1, C2

Parish of St. George, C4, D4
Parish of St. John, C4, C5, D4, D5
Parish of St. Mary, C4, C5
Parish of St. Paul, C5, D5
Parish of St. Peter, D4, D5
Parish of St. Philip, D4, D5
Pelican Bay, D1, D2
Pillar Book Bay, C4
Potworks Dam, D4, D5

Redonda, A5

Salt Pond, D2

St. John's, C4

Two Feet Bay, D1

Wallings Forest, C5
Willikies, D4
Willoughby Bay, D5

# ECONOMIC ANTIGUA AND BARBUDA

## Industry

Crayfish

Dockyard

Factory

Sand

## Agriculture

Pineapple &
Bananas

Pumpkin &
Sweet potatoes

## Services

Airport

Tourism

# ABOUT THE ECONOMY

*All figures are 2019 estimates unless otherwise noted.*

**GROSS DOMESTIC PRODUCT (GDP, OFFICIAL EXCHANGE RATE)**
$1.662 billion

**GDP PER CAPITA (BASED ON PURCHASING POWER PARITY)**
$17,113

**GDP SECTORS**
agriculture 1.8 percent, industry 20.8 percent, services 77.3 percent (2017)

**LAND AREA**
170 square miles (442 sq km)

**AGRICULTURAL PRODUCTS**
tropical fruit, milk, mangoes and guavas, melons, tomatoes, pineapples, lemons, limes, eggplants, onions

**INDUSTRIES**
tourism, construction, light manufacturing (clothing, alcohol, household appliances)

**UNEMPLOYMENT RATE**
11 percent (2014)

**CURRENCY**
1 Eastern Caribbean dollar (XCD) = 100 cents
notes: 5, 10, 20, 50, 100 dollars
coins: 1, 2, 5, 10, 25 cents; 1 dollar
$1 USD = 2.70 XCD (January 2021)

**MAIN EXPORTS**
ships, refined petroleum, precious/semi-precious metal scraps, rice, corn

**MAIN IMPORTS**
refined petroleum, ships, cars, precious/semi-precious metals, recreational boats

**TRADE PARTNERS**
United States, Poland, Cameroon, United Kingdom, Spain

**INTERNATIONAL AIRPORT**
V. C. Bird International Airport (Saint John's)

**PORTS AND HARBORS**
Deepwater Harbour, English Harbour, Jolly Harbour, Falmouth Harbour, Port Harbour

# CULTURAL
# ANTIGUA AND BARBUDA

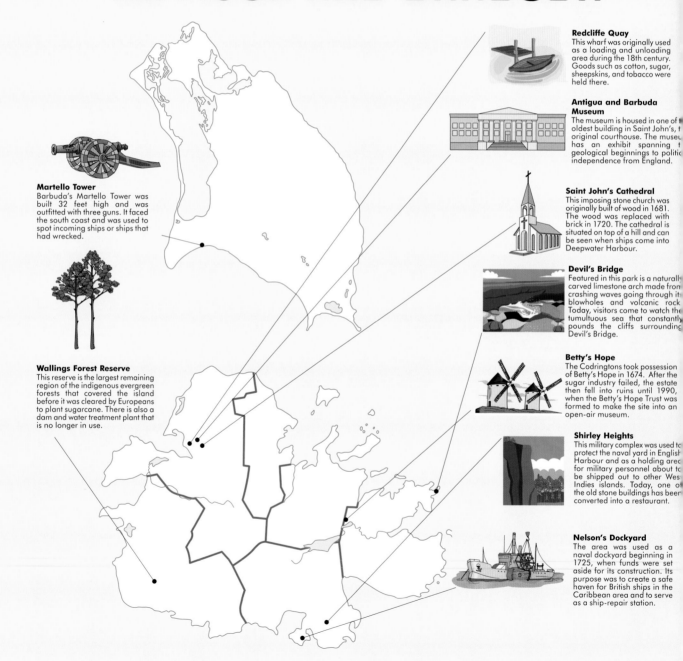

**Redcliffe Quay**
This wharf was originally used as a loading and unloading area during the 18th century. Goods such as cotton, sugar, sheepskins, and tobacco were held there.

**Antigua and Barbuda Museum**
The museum is housed in one of the oldest building in Saint John's, the original courthouse. The museum has an exhibit spanning the geological beginnings to political independence from England.

**Saint John's Cathedral**
This imposing stone church was originally built of wood in 1681. The wood was replaced with brick in 1720. The cathedral is situated on top of a hill and can be seen when ships come into Deepwater Harbour.

**Devil's Bridge**
Featured in this park is a naturally carved limestone arch made from crashing waves going through it, blowholes and volcanic rock. Today, visitors come to watch the tumultuous sea that constantly pounds the cliffs surrounding Devil's Bridge.

**Betty's Hope**
The Codringtons took possession of Betty's Hope in 1674. After the sugar industry failed, the estate then fell into ruins until 1990, when the Betty's Hope Trust was formed to make the site into an open-air museum.

**Shirley Heights**
This military complex was used to protect the naval yard in English Harbour and as a holding area for military personnel about to be shipped out to other West Indies islands. Today, one of the old stone buildings has been converted into a restaurant.

**Nelson's Dockyard**
The area was used as a naval dockyard beginning in 1725, when funds were set aside for its construction. Its purpose was to create a safe haven for British ships in the Caribbean area and to serve as a ship-repair station.

**Martello Tower**
Barbuda's Martello Tower was built 32 feet high and was outfitted with three guns. It faced the south coast and was used to spot incoming ships or ships that had wrecked.

**Wallings Forest Reserve**
This reserve is the largest remaining region of the indigenous evergreen forests that covered the island before it was cleared by Europeans to plant sugarcane. There is also a dam and water treatment plant that is no longer in use.

# ABOUT THE CULTURE

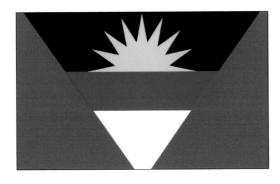

*All figures are 2021 estimates unless otherwise noted.*

**OFFICAL NAME**
Antigua and Barbuda

**CAPITAL**
Saint John's

**OTHER IMPORTANT CITIES**
Codrington

**POPULATION**
99,175

**POPULATION GROWTH RATE**
1.17 percent

**BIRTH RATE**
15.3 births per 1,000 people

**LIFE EXPECTANCY AT BIRTH**
total population: 77.55 years
male: 75.37 years
female: 79.85 years

**ETHNIC GROUPS**
African descent 87.3 percent, mixed 4.7 percent, Hispanic 2.7 percent, white 1.6 percent, other 2.7 percent, unspecified 0.9 percent (2011)

**LANGUAGES**
English (official), Antiguan Creole

**RELIGIOUS GROUPS**
Protestant 68.3 percent (Anglican 17.6 percent, Seventh-day Adventist 12.4 percent, Pentecostal 12.2 percent, Moravian 8.3 percent, Methodist 5.6 percent, Wesleyan Holiness 4.5 percent, Church of God 4.1 percent, Baptist 3.6 percent), Roman Catholic 8.2 percent, other 12.2 percent, unspecified 5.5 percent, none 5.9 percent (2011)

**URBAN POPULATION**
24.4 percent (2020)

**ADMINISTRATIVE DIVISIONS**
Parishes: Saint George, Saint John, Saint Mary, Saint Paul, Saint Peter, Saint Philip Dependencies: Barbuda, Redonda

**LITERACY RATE**
99 percent (2015)

# TIMELINE

| IN ANTIGUA AND BARBUDA | IN THE WORLD |
|---|---|
| **3000 BCE** Stone Age people populate Barbuda. | |
| **775 BCE** The Ceramic Age starts slowly in Antigua. Arawak farmers arrive from Venezuela. | |
| | **753 BCE** Rome is founded. |
| | **600 CE** The height of the Maya civilization is reached. |
| **1493 CE** Antigua is claimed for Spain by Columbus and named Santa Maria la Antigua. | |
| | **1530** The transatlantic slave trade begins. |
| | **1620** Pilgrims sail the *Mayflower* to America. |
| **1632** Antigua becomes an English colony led by Sir Thomas Warner. | |
| **1674** Sir Christopher Codrington establishes a large sugar plantation on Antigua. | |
| **1678** Barbuda becomes an English colony. | |
| **1685** The Codringtons lease the island of Barbuda. | |
| **1689–1698** Christopher Codrington serves as the governor of Antigua. | |
| | **1776** The U.S. Declaration of Independence is written. |
| **1785–1792** The majority of the buildings seen today in English Harbour are built. | |
| | **1789–1799** The French Revolution takes place. |
| **1834** Slavery in Antigua and Barbuda is abolished. | |
| **1870** Barbuda is united with Antigua. | **1861** The American Civil War begins. |
| | **1914** World War I begins. |
| **1939** Antigua Trades and Labour Union is founded. | **1939–1945** World War II devastates Europe. |
| **1943** Vere Cornwall Bird is elected president of the Antigua Trades and Labour Union. | **1945** The North Atlantic Treaty Organization (NATO) is formed. |

| IN ANTIGUA AND BARBUDA | | IN THE WORLD |
|---|---|---|
| | **1957** | |
| **1958–1962** | | The Russians launch *Sputnik*. |
| Antigua is part of the Federation of the West Indies. | **1966–1969** | The Chinese Cultural Revolution takes place. |
| | **1969** | U.S. astronaut Neil Armstrong becomes the first human on the moon. |
| **1981** | | |
| Antigua and Barbuda wins independence; V. C. Bird is the first prime minister. | **1986** | A nuclear power disaster occurs at Chernobyl in Ukraine. |
| | **1991** | The breakup of the Soviet Union takes place. |
| | **2001** | |
| **2004** | | Terrorists attack the United States on 9/11. |
| Baldwin Spencer becomes prime minister. | | |
| **2007** | | |
| Antigua and Barbuda cohosts Cricket World Cup. | | |
| **2008** | **2008** | |
| The tourism industry is rocked by the shooting of a British honeymooning couple. | | Americans elect their first African American president, Barack Obama. |
| **2009** | **2009** | |
| Allen Stanford is charged with massive investment fraud. | | An outbreak of H1N1 flu spreads around the world. |
| **2013** | | |
| The government launches a scheme allowing foreigners to purchase citizenship. | | |
| **2014** | | |
| Antigua Labour Party (ALP) wins general elections; Gaston Browne becomes prime minister. | **2015–2016** | ISIS launches terror attacks in Belgium and France. |
| **2017** | **2017** | |
| Hurricane Irma devastates Barbuda. | | Donald Trump becomes U.S. president. |
| | **2019** | Notre Dame Cathedral in Paris is damaged by fire. |
| **2020–2021** | **2020** | |
| The COVID-19 pandemic drastically hurts tourism in Antigua and Barbuda. | | The COVID-19 pandemic spreads across the world. |
| | **2021** | Joe Biden becomes president of the United States. |

# GLOSSARY

**benna**
A traditional folksong genre associated with Antigua and Barbuda.

**Caribana**
A Carnival celebration on Barbuda.

**cassava**
An edible, starchy root.

**coral reefs**
Underwater limestone structures made of coral animals.

**corruption**
Dishonest or illegal behavior, especially by powerful people, such as government officials.

**desalination**
The process of purifying salt or brackish water by removing the dissolved salts.

**fungee**
A cornmeal dumpling or mush with okra.

**money laundering**
Disguising money earned from criminal activities.

**Obeah**
A form of sorcery brought from West Africa.

**offshore banking**
A type of banking that allows a person or a corporation to set up a bank account and keep information about the contents and transactions of that account confidential.

**pepperpot**
A stew of meats and vegetables popular throughout the Caribbean.

**regatta**
A series of boat races.

**visiting union**
A family arrangement in which a man and woman have children together, but live in different locations.

**Wadadli**
The traditional name for the island of Antigua.

# FOR FURTHER INFORMATION

## BOOKS

Insight Guides. *Antigua and Barbuda Pocket Guide*. London, UK: Insight Guides, 2019.

Kincaid, Jamaica. *A Small Place*. New York, NY: Farrar, Straus and Giroux, 2000.

Lightfoot, Natasha. *Troubling Freedom: Antigua and the Aftermath of British Emancipation*. Durham, NC: Duke University Press, 2015.

## ONLINE

Antigua and Barbuda Government Information and Services. ab.gov.ag.

Antigua Nice. antiguanice.com.

Barbudaful. www.barbudaful.net.

*Britannica*. "Antigua and Barbuda." www.britannica.com/place/Antigua-and-Barbuda.

CIA. *The World Factbook*. "Antigua and Barbuda." www.cia.gov/the-world-factbook/countries/antigua-and-barbuda.

*The Daily Observer*. www.antiguaobserver.com.

## MUSIC

King Short Shirt. *Carnival In Antigua 2017*, Vp Records, 2017.

# BIBLIOGRAPHY

ABHTA. "Resorts on Antigua & Barbuda Offer On-Site Antigen Testing for UK and US Guests." Antigua and Barbuda Hotels and Tourism Association, January 26, 2021. visitantiguabarbuda.com/press.

Antigua Nice. antiguanice.com.

BBC News. "Antigua and Barbuda Country Profile." www.bbc.com/news/world-latin-america-18706079.

BBC News. "Antigua and Barbuda profile—Timeline." www.bbc.com/news/world-latin-america-18707512.

*Britannica.* "Antigua and Barbuda." www.britannica.com/place/Antigua-and-Barbuda.

*Caribbean Journal.* "Antigua and Barbuda Sets a New Tourism Record." January 1, 2020. www.caribjournal.com/2020/01/01/antigua-and-barbuda-tourism-milestone.

CIA. *The World Factbook.* "Antigua and Barbuda." www.cia.gov/the-world-factbook/countries/antigua-and-barbuda.

Drake, Monica. "Jamaica Kincaid's Antigua." *New York Times*, July 13, 2016. www.nytimes.com/2016/07/17/travel/antigua-jamaica-kincaid.html.

Gore-Francis, Janil. "Antigua and Barbuda: SIDS 2014 Preparatory Progress Report." Ministry of Agriculture, Housing, Lands, and the Environment, July 2013. sustainabledevelopment.un.org/content/documents/1049240Antigua percent20and percent20Barbuda percent20final.pdf.

Handy, Gemma. "Antigua: Sprawling 'Chinese Colony' Plan Across Marine Reserve Ignites Opposition." *The Guardian*, June 20, 2019. www.theguardian.com/world/2019/jun/20/antigua-yida-project-chinese-colony-controversy.

Hassan, Adeel. "Antigua Demands Harvard Pay Reparations for Benefiting From Slavery." *New York Times*, November 6, 2019. www.nytimes.com/2019/11/06/us/harvard-antigua-slavery-reparations.html.

Hopegood, Rosie. "Lockdown in paradise: Antigua's plea for visitors." *Al Jazeera*, November 8, 2020. www.aljazeera.com/features/2020/11/8/lockdown-in-paradise-antiguas-plea-for.

Kaufman, Michael T. "Vere Bird, 89, Who Led Antigua to Freedom," *New York Times*, June 30, 1999. www.nytimes.com/1999/06/30/world/vere-bird-89-who-led-antigua-to-freedom.html.

National Hurricane Center. "Tropical Cyclone Report: Hurricane Irma." June 30, 2018. www.nhc.noaa.gov/data/tcr/AL112017_Irma.pdf.

Pressly, Linda. "Why I Don't Want to Own the Land My Business Is Built On." BBC News, August 14, 2019. www.bbc.com/news/stories-49210150.

*The Daily Observer.* www.antiguaobserver.com.

World Atlas. "Antigua and Barbuda." www.worldatlas.com/webimage/countrys/namerica/caribb/ag.htm.

# INDEX

**143**

# INDEX